Proverbial
#TWEETS

10 YEARS OF PUBLIC AND PRIVATE FAITH

ALISA HOPE WAGNER

Marked Writers Publishing

Proverbial
#TWEETS

10 YEARS OF PUBLIC AND PRIVATE FAITH

#DEDICATION

I offer this book to all the people out there who are recklessly chasing after their God-given promises. May your faith be encouraged and your strength renewed.

I want to thank my husband, Daniel, for all of his support. And to my children—Isaac, Levi and Kiki—you inspire all that I do.

Also, thank you to my sister, Shay, for painstakingly copying all my tweets and to Patricia Coughlin and Faith Newton for your kind edits. And to Holly for giving me yet another book idea.

Finally, I am in awe that God would use me to further His Kingdom on earth as it is in heaven. I'm honored to be called Your daughter.

#PROLOGUE

My friend sent me a text with an image of a Bible study that her husband and son were doing together. The author of the book had quoted one of my tweets.

> *"Surrender is the only path to supernatural living." – Alisa Hope Wagner.*

I decided right away that I needed to put my tweets in a book. I have been publicizing my faith for over 10 years, and I didn't want those moments to fade away. Those declarations were my way of encouraging myself in the Lord.

After getting all of my tweets, I thought it would be interesting to parallel my public statements with my inner struggles and victories. I've journaled my thoughts since I was fourteen, so I gathered many of my handwritten words from the last ten years and typed them in this book. I didn't document all of them, but I did bring forth my cries to the Lord—cries of heartache, hope, frustration and expectancy.

It is so easy to look at social media and think someone has it all together. But what I've learned is that we all are walking down a path of reliance on the Lord.

We all have deep yearnings that God has given us, but the one desire He wants us to have most is a need to love and be loved by Him.

A transformation can be seen as the ten years quickly transpire within this book. My faith that was once superficial has become more resilient. My passion for God's promises are just as strong, but now my passion for Him is stronger.

I decided to have the book go backward, starting with my most recent tweets and moving to when my tweets began ten years ago. That way the readers can see my faith as it stands today and journey the years of refining in rewind. Sometimes it's better to see the grandeur from the peak before starting the slow trek up the mountain.

Although I am still waiting for many of God's promises, I have learned to rest in Him. It is a difficult thing to wait with a God-given dream. God's ways are not our own, and we must wander the wilderness for many years before reaching our Promised Land. But it is in the desert places where we truly learn to rely on God.

All of our stories will be different, but we will all have to learn to wait for our promises. I believe waiting on God and trusting in His timing is one of the most difficult things for a Christian to learn. Sometimes hope can feel like a burden, especially when it stretches over years of expectancy. However, the wisdom, understanding and refining we gain during the years of waiting are more valuable than gold.

I encourage you to never give up. Hold onto your faith and believe God at His word. What He has spoken over your life will come to pass.

Regardless of your circumstances, no matter if your promises seem dead, trust God and wait with anticipation. Your faith is priceless.

> *"Faith shows the reality of what we hope for; it is the evidence of things we cannot see" (Hebrews 11.1 NLT).*

#YEAR 10

"Hope deferred makes the heart sick, but a dream fulfilled is a tree of life" (Proverbs 13.12 NLT).

God wants to produce faith in us. Our entire relationship with Him and all of His promises hinge on that single word, *faith*. Producing faith means that we must also carry the burden of hope. Hope can become quite heavy as we wait upon God. And every unfulfilled promise we carry causes hope to multiply and gain weight. After years of believing and waiting, hope can feel like an oppressive burden. However, we must remember that faith is the fertile soil where God's supernatural promises are grown. Don't ever give up—even when all seems lost. God will bring life into what feels dead.

@Public

Sometimes God will allow you to lose everything, so you can finally make your way to Him.

Your destiny depends on your obedience!

People want to see an interactive God, so share what He's doing in your life.

Never put limits on a limitless God.

You know you're a writer when you are trying to edit your book, but you start getting caught up in the story and lose your place.

I can't wait until my Young Adult Fantasy book is published, so my kids can read it and finally realize that mommy is actually working when she gets to "sit in front of the computer all day."

When we are not firmly in God each day, we become an easy target for distraction. That's why quiet times with Him are so important!

I could spend endless hours editing a book, but there has to come that moment when you say, "I'm done. If a typo has worked this hard to stay hidden, it deserves to be published."

The bad thing about being sick is that I can't exercise. The good thing about being sick is that I'm getting a lot of writing and editing done. Even so, I'd rather be feeling 100% and in the gym!

> WE CAN'T BE EVERYTHING TO EVERYONE, BUT WE CAN BE OURSELVES TO A SELECT FEW.

The one thing I love about hamburger soup is that you don't need a recipe — just culinary gusto!

God uses the rejection of others to propel you in the direction He wants you to go.

So many walls that God wants to tear down because they separate us from His peace and joy, and most of those walls are inside of us, not our circumstances.

By faith...By faith...By faith we achieve all that God has planned for us. This means we believe in His promises with no proof, walking in faith towards the goal knowing that it is impossible yet believing and moving anyway.

It's a difficult place when God breaks you down, but it's a necessary step to fulfilling your destiny.

When my feelings contradict God's Word, I go by what I know to be true, not what feels true.

Thinking about aging, so I wrote a little fiction piece. I am always aware that this life is precious, yet fleeting. "Soothing light embraces the bulbous blooms saddened that their cresting beauty diminishes in fading rays, as one by one pink petals fall to their glassy graves."

"And Abraham named that place The Lord Will Provide"(Gen. 22.14). Is there an area of your life that you need provision? Don't look to people and things; look to the Provider! Go to Him in prayer and stand in complete faith, claiming with full belief: "The Lord Will Provide!"

I don't want to look back on my life and realize just how much the enemy stole my joy. I have a joy that's dependent on nothing other than the love of God through Jesus.

Have you ever had something so important to do, and you do all the minor to-dos on your list around it until finally you have no choice but to do it because it's all you have left to do?

Life would be easier if I chose only one genre to write, but life would also be more boring.

"God desires so much to be a part of our lives that He chose to create three embodiments of His Person, so no matter where we turn, He is there with us." – from my one-year devotional, Slay the Day

Do everything in your power to right the situation and bring out justice, and when you're done, leave the rest in God's hands and dispatch the anger, frustration and disappointment to Him. It's not worth carrying.

A lot of our stress and worry would disappear if we would simply tell God, "It is well with my soul."

I'm so fascinated by every aspect of God's creation! I want to write everything that inspires me in a book. But the list is running long and time is running short.

God wants to fulfill your promises, but He wants you to learn to love and be loved by Him first.

Doing something well always takes an investment of time, resources and energy. Cutting corners only leads to more work in the end.

I feel so honored to be a steward of people's words.

Fill yourself so much with God's Word and what He says about you that there is no room left for doubt. Shape your destiny with faith, not fear!

I choose respect over offense. And prayer over shouting.

When you take a step of faith, you willingly face possible failure, rejection and embarrassment, but you trust God so much that His word usurps your fears.

No goal comes without obstacles. No destiny without hardships.

The deadlines you make for yourself are the hardest to keep because you alone are accountable.

Sometimes I set writing goals that make me wonder if my mind is truly set in reality.

I'm reading through Genesis, and I just finished chapter 4. I find it fascinating that so far only three jobs have been listed. 1) Working the ground. 2) Working with livestock. And 3) Working with instruments. The value of music should never be underestimated.

Your willingness to be rejected will help you find opportunities that most people will never see.

Any time you start making strides away from your strongholds and toward your destiny, Satan will attack you. Just consider your trials a confirmation that you're on the right track.

It's so tempting to dive into my pile of to-dos. But I know that prayer, Bible reading and time with God will establish my day in Christ, making my efforts more effective, efficient and eternal.

People who judge so easily probably have no idea how much work is involved.

Just as a fiction writer creates characters and places great value in them. God created you and places great value in you. Why? Because

He created you to be an integral part of His Kingdom Story. Find your place in this Great Story and you'll find your purpose.

Your destiny is too big to navigate alone. Without prayer and the Bible you will get lost in the minutiae.

I want every thought and action I make today to be submitted to the Holy Spirit and done according to God's Kingdom Plan, which does include rest and play done purposefully. Life is fleeting, and I want to make all my special moments on earth count now and for eternity.

Staying fit would be so much easier if my job and destiny didn't call for me to sit for hours of the day typing on the computer.

You must be your biggest advocate by believing God's promises for your life and taking actions of faith.

I'm just amazed by God! He asks you to do some crazy faith dream, but then He directs you to the simplest steps along the way.

> WE WILL NEVER ACHIEVE OUR DESTINY UNLESS WE GO THROUGH THE TRIALS THAT PUSH US THERE.

Whatever you're struggling with today just remember God has a bigger plan. Instead of hyper-focusing on the problem, comprehend the mighty strength and the all-consuming power of a God who absolutely adores you.

When we stop trying to be someone we're not, we'll fall in love with the person we are.

We lack God's power because we lack the presence of His Son. Only Jesus unleashes the Holy Spirit. Only Jesus brings forth rivers of Living Water.

God sent His Son to die for us, so He can have communication with us!

Every time I finish writing a book, I jot down two more that I want to write. I have a sneaking suspicion that the list doesn't end.

"We cannot trust the circumstances around us because God moves in an atmosphere far above our comprehension." - Slay the Day: Your Daily Dose of Victory

May we never get so advanced and so smart in our field of study that we stop relying on God to guide us. We may be able to climb a mountain with our own strength and ingenuity, but we will never move it. Only childlike faith makes the impossible possible.

Just a little reminder for all of us today. It is not by our power or our might but by God's Spirit alone. What releases God's Spirit? Jesus. Rest in Him and let God work in your obedience (Zechariah 4:6).

The enemy will do everything possible to make you give up right before God unleashes His breakthrough in your life. Stand firm on faith, muster your courage and wait on God. He will come through!

It's easy to hold our hands up on stage before the crowds to the Lord, but will we still hold them up in the pit of obscurity to Him?

When we learn to do something with excellence when no one is looking, we will truly know what it means to work for the Lord and not human masters of applause, fame and attention.

Criticizers base their opinions on perfection. Encouragers base their opinions on excellence. Do your very best and God will do the rest!

What does the life of faith truly look like? And how would it play out in a dystopian, alternate reality where America has fallen and two diverse people groups arise? Find out in my Onoma Series, starting with the first book, Eve of Awakening!

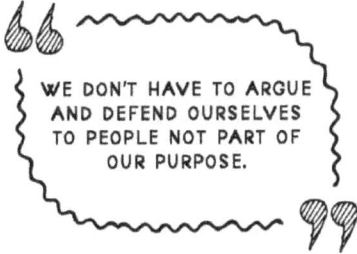

> WE DON'T HAVE TO ARGUE AND DEFEND OURSELVES TO PEOPLE NOT PART OF OUR PURPOSE.

When we are not rooted firmly in God, we become easy targets for distraction.

Writers have a special place in my heart. We may be sensitive and weird, but we are excellent at expressing it.

Someone may have your heart's longing, but you may have something they desire. No one has it all, but we all have the One who provides us with complete joy, peace and love.

Free will requires us to be attentive to the Holy Spirit's movements in our lives. God nudges our hearts in tender moments, and if we are rushed and distracted, we can miss it.

Don't let your lack, other people or your own mind cause you to stop doing what God has called you to do. Press through. Don't give up. Keep at it. And in His chosen season, God will move through your faith!

Let us never become so critical that we miss the beauty in ourselves and others. Instead of fault-finding, we can be good-seeking.

God must change you first, so you can change the world.

When you follow God to a shut door, you have to trust that it's merely a divine detour.

The dream that God puts inside of us is like a baby. We must give our energy, time and resources for years without expecting anything in return. Many people abandon their dreams because they are so small and helpless. People can't see the mighty harvest the dream will become.

It's hard to fill others with value if you haven't filled yourself with God's value first. Everything you give must be received, so you can give from an overflow.

I pray for a divine thorn in all of our sides that makes us aware of our need and fully reliant on and humble to the Holy Spirit.

Be a student of the Holy Spirit, and He will lead you in all the knowledge you need to achieve the destiny He's designed for you.

People are allowed their own opinions, but if their words contradict what God has spoken into your life, rebuke and dismiss them quickly. Never, ever harbor lies.

Don't let your past mistakes cause you to miss your future blessings.

It takes hours to write an article, seconds to submit it and a lifetime to hear back from the publisher. I have so many articles submitted that I've lost count. You never know which one will bite.

Christian writers make the walk of faith possible to others because they have made it imaginable to them.

May the hidden areas of my life be just as beautiful and faithful as the areas I choose to show.

On the other side of our confession, is healing. On the other side of our humility, is blessing. On the other side of our forgiveness, is freedom. We have just a brief moment in every decision to choose the higher reaction of the Spirit where God's goodness is displayed.

The only way to truly get really good at what you do is to pour in all the hours and to make all the mistakes.

That very thing you've been searching for outside of you might be the very same thing that God's trying to produce within you.

I'm fulling understanding that anxiety is a sin, and it builds a wall between God and me because I am not trusting Him. He knows what I need. He knows the beginning to the end. I will do my part and wait on Him.

OUR FAILURES DON'T FORFEIT GOD'S FAITHFULNESS.

Many times the fruit of our labor cannot be seen on the outside because it is growing on the inside. God usually does an internal work before He makes an external change.

It's not defeat when you've done everything you can in your own strength, and you choose to leave the rest in God's hands. It's trust.

Give your negative thoughts to God and He will give you His thoughts of truth—acceptance, joy, peace, life, love and hope.

Victories that are clean-cut and easy are not worth the fight. We should be dragging ourselves by pure determination and grit across the finish line of the victories that truly matter.

Never let your mind dwell on bitterness. Process the hurt and allow it to make you wiser and stronger. Determine to treat people better than how you have been treated and give room for God to give you His thoughts of goodness, peace and joy!

Jesus' unending love for you is always consistent.

Words can't hurt if you put more faith in how God sees you than how others see you.

Pour your faith into every new point of disappointment, rejection and offense, so that God can make you stronger, empowering you to love others without expectation or reimbursement.

It's a good place to be when against all odds and after years of waiting and working that you choose to have faith instead of fear and trust instead of doubt, believing God is good because of His Word and not your circumstances.

The sins you are stuck in are substitutes for the giftings that God has called you to. Find your destiny and the shackles of sin will fall.

Replace your doubt with daring; your worry with wonder; and your fear with faith! Choose to trust God and be in awe of what He's doing even when it doesn't make sense!

Greatness rests on God's favor poured over your persistence.

Ask God to show you who you really are, so you don't have to struggle with who you are not.

Sometimes it's better to go after what you really want than "cover all the bases." What are you desiring today? How are you chasing your dreams?

God's faithfulness is the armor protecting you from doubt when the enemy tries to make you question God's promises in your life!!!

Every time hope gets deferred in your life, fill the void with faith. Eventually you'll be surrounded by thick layers of faith for Jesus to break through and shine His glory. *based on my favorite verse, Proverbs 13.12

God is the ultimate mover and shaper of your fate. Do all you can in your strength in obedience to the Holy Spirit and then rest in the resurrection power of Jesus.

You grow in the struggle. You lean into God from the force. You find yourself in Him after feeling lost. You thrive against the winds of resistance.

Don't be nervous or afraid! If God has called you to do something that is beyond your current ability, He will supply all you need to obey His command! Just take the first step and trust His provision of grace, favor, knowledge and strength!

> NEVER MOVE OUT OF FEAR. ALWAYS MOVE OUT OF FAITH IN THE LOVE, AUTHORITY AND PURPOSE THAT GOD HAS GIFTED YOU.

God is so big that He engulfs your problems. Nothing surprises Him, and He always has a plan for your good and the completion of His Kingdom on earth as it is in Heaven.

You can try to take the writer out of the story, but you can't take the story out of the writer.

The grace of Jesus not only saves us, it gives us the power to walk according to His ways.

When God places someone on your heart, drop everything you're doing and pray for them in the spirit.

Walk by faith in the victory that God has already given you even when you can't perceive it just yet.

When the devil has you in check, God already has him in checkmate.

When we remember just how big God is, we are reminded how small our problems are in His hands.

No matter your circumstances and the odds against you, cry out to God, and He will have the final victory.

MOVE OUT OF FAITH, NOT FEAR!

It takes faith to anticipate a move of God and to prepare in the wilderness for the Promised Land, but God is faithful to the promises He has given you!

When God searches the depths of your heart and soul, He is looking for only one thing: love for His Son, Jesus Christ, the Messiah and Savior of the world.

It's scary and thrilling when God gives you Scripture to write about, but you have no idea what He wants you to say. That's when you know the Holy Spirit has to come through for you. Just start typing and the words will come!

I've learned to keep my eyes open and my ears alert. God is a masterful story weaver. He wouldn't waste one single detail in the chapters of your life and the fruition of His Kingdom on earth as it is in heaven.

There's revelation that God gives you that He expects you to serve. However, there is revelation that He gives you for your benefit and wellbeing alone. We can seek both personal and platform revelation, filling others as well as ourselves.

Believe in yourself even when others don't. Your promises are between you and God, not you and the world.

I am declaring Ezekiel 34.29-31 over myself today! Read God's Word and proclaim the promises that the Holy Spirit highlights in your life today for the circumstances around you and the needs within you!

Never let the opinions of others sidetrack you from all that God has prepared for you. Really focus on the words you allow yourself to absorb. Block everything that does not align with how God sees you and how He created you.

Never become stagnant in who you think God has called you to be. He can always call out more. You can always rise up in different ways. Your story can always have more plot twists and surprises!

If you believe you are going to heaven through the death and the resurrection of Jesus, you must then also believe that you have been made clean.

I finished three sets of edits to my book. I'm so appreciative to my sweet family and friends who took time to pour into my book. Just a few more rounds of edits to go!

Put all your value and worth in who you are in Christ and how God sees and loves you, and you will rise above the sting of rejection from others.

Grace is our access point to God!

God can make the foolish areas of our lives wise and the weakest parts of our character strong. Never underestimate what He can accomplish in a faithful, willing heart.

God's fruit can do no wrong!

I love to purposely leave loose ends at the beginning of my book only to tie them into the end.

Jesus was forsaken, so we wouldn't be!

To have someone believe in you and God's promises for your life by faith, not by sight, is a powerful thing!

Claim God's promises even when all circumstances scream at you to doubt His Word.

No matter how divided the Church becomes, we are on the winning side of history and time if we believe and live the Gospel of Jesus Christ.

The beauty or ugliness and the faith or fear inside of you is revealed when circumstances and people squeeze you.

When you love the calling God has designed for your life, you will place great value on all that you do, regardless of what other people think. God has given you a special purpose and your life has profound meaning.

If you can stay motivated by God's Word alone and His promises for your life (regardless of your circumstances), you will produce great faith and works for His glory.

Jesus was angered that His "Father's House" was made into a marketplace. I wonder how many churches today are running like businesses rather than God's Home with His family.

You have to change your thinking to match your desired circumstance. The inner person dictates the outer situation.

Give your sweat equity of faith to Jesus, and He will turn your plain water into His best wine. He will perform a miracle in your works of obedience.

Desperation for a move or miracle of God forces us to let go of human tradition and move beyond the expectation of others.

Prepare for God's promises by faith despite how you feel and your current circumstances and trust that Jesus will show up in your obedience!

I'm amazed that when I'm not rushed or distracted, God is easily able to prepare me for each day's needs.

Cutting the links of unforgiveness is like cutting the chains that have kept you held down. Let the bitterness go and watch yourself rise up!

I choose a spirit of forgiveness over a spirit of bitterness, a spirit of thankfulness over a spirit of poverty and a spirit of faith over a spirit of fear.

I am starting my day with an attitude of thankfulness, listing the myriad of blessings God gives me each day. A spirit of thankfulness disperses the spirit of lack.

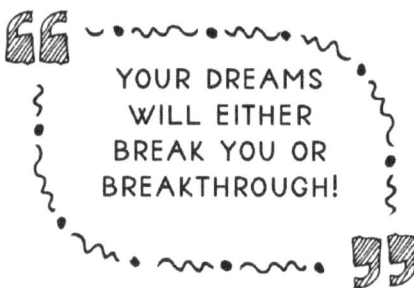

> YOUR DREAMS WILL EITHER BREAK YOU OR BREAKTHROUGH!

I talk about Jesus not because I am perfect, but He is. Your chipped and misshapen vessel doesn't limit the power of a Holy God. He can flow through anyone who's willing.

The spirit of thankfulness devours the spirit of lack.

God loves to see our faith in His promises. Never give up believing even when all circumstances tell you it's hopeless. God is bigger than your situation.

We have been made holy and righteous through Jesus Christ. Once we fully believe and embrace this truth, we will begin to live it out in our daily lives. Belief activates action.

We are stewards of the destiny God has given each of us. Jesus is our Morning Star to guide us each day on our journey.

You don't have to do everything. Just do the things that make your spirit soar. I love working out, writing and spending time with my husband, kids and God!

Do something today without pay, without credit and without applause, and watch how God blesses you.

Sometimes you don't know the greatness you have stored in you until circumstance pushes it out.

Don't let pride cause you to regret or even dismiss God's favor. You're His child. Let Him accomplish for you what you could never achieve on your own.

We have to stop looking to others for our confirmation and start looking to God. He is our breakthrough.

The challenge of something makes the victory sweeter.

The easiest way to love people unconditionally is to not throw your expectations on them.

Don't fear sin. Jesus has already overcome them. When people make mistakes, remind them that Jesus has given them the victory. They've already won.

It is impossible to establish God's commands in your heart when others are constantly trying to establish them for you.

> **THE UNEXPECTED MOVE OF GOD IS BUILT ON YEARS OF SACRIFICE, OBEDIENCE AND FAITH.**

God will put you in the crowds to minister to others for a season, and He will separate you from the crowds to minister to you personally for a season. Both are crucial.

Pray for those in authority of your life. You will only rise as they do.

Wait on the hope of something better rather than settle on the reality of something mediocre.

The only thing your future blessings are waiting on is for you to bring your thoughts and actions in agreement with them.

Choose today to identify and replace one negative thought pattern with a thought of God's acceptance, love and abundance.

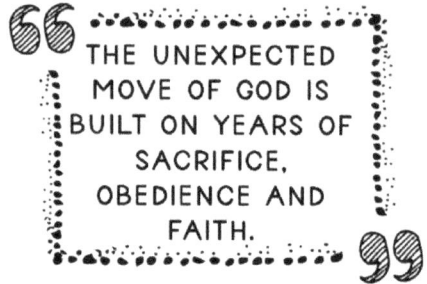

@Private

There is life in salvation through Jesus Christ. But there is also life or resurrection in our promises for those of us willing to die and be reborn, letting our promises die and be reborn. I love You, God. I will not fear. I will not doubt. I will believe. I will trust. I will pour out my faith to You. I believe Your promises. Your promises are sure and true. Your great arm is not short. There is so much harvest. Let me be Your harvester. Give me land and the lower and upper springs. I will stand strong in God. You know what the world needs. Help me to fulfill that need.

―――――――――

Be a person that pours confidence, endurance and joy into others. When we are offended by someone else's gifting, we become jealous and condemn them for what we can't do. Lord, let me never be offended! Your arm is long and strong for all of us! I know You have blessed me much. I have an amazing husband, awesome kids and a lifestyle that is blessed. But my platform is dead. Your promises to me are dead in the natural. Please resurrect Your promises to me. I ask You by faith to redeem my obedience and faith steps. I am undeserving and maybe my books are not as good and deserving, but I ask that You bring my platform to life and spread Your banner over me. My writing is ready and waiting for Jesus to come. He will come like a thief. Lord, I am ready. My books are ready. The Upper Room is furnished and waiting for You. Please send Your Spirit and let it fall onto my writing.

―――――――――

Today, I am reading Genesis 9, and God is blessing Noah. He worked on the Ark preparing for the rains by faith. I've worked on my books preparing by faith for You to send the rains. I see Your promises. I experienced the double portion of Your law. Now bless me with Your rains. I will use my platform to raise up voices. I trust You. Rejection from people hurts, but I will never be rejected by You, Lord! You shine Your face upon me. You are pleased with me. You give me a double portion, and after all these years, I am still here. Birds of prey have constantly tried to devour my books, but I stay vigilant shooing them away.

Lord, instead of having to move me away from destruction because of my lack of faith, I know that I've lived on faith. Faith so pleases You. You will move my books toward prosperity. Grab hold of every single one and move them into people's hands. It was out of bondage that Israel became rich. It was out of extreme oppression that God poured out His favor. Let God bring you into such an oppressive and desolate place that He will rise up and defend and protect you Himself. It's been almost thirteen years since I wrote my first book. Prosper my work, Lord, and the words of my heart.

Lord, I have traveled the writing road for so long. The streets have multiplied before me all going the same way. I'm cultivating dozens of paths, but there is no end in sight. How will You tie all of the streams together? Will You pour Your abundance and favor into all of my books? Are they all valuable in Your sight? When will You show up in my work and my efforts of faith? I need a miracle. I've stepped out on faith, believing You would prosper my books from day one. They are all published and waiting for you—twenty-two books. I love You, Lord. I've given You every single ounce of faith that I have left in me. January 2019 will be thirteen years since I started this journey. I am tired, and I need Your supernatural help and to be worthy of You through Jesus.

#YEAR 9

"And they have defeated him by the blood of the Lamb and by their testimony. And they did not love their lives so much that they were afraid to die" (Revelation 12.11 NLT).

The Blood of Jesus Christ is the supernatural power that redeems and resurrects our life and steps of obedience. Some people try to depict blood as something grotesque and taboo. The reality, though, is that blood is the life essence of a living thing. So when we contemplate the Blood of Jesus, we can envision the life essence of God in the Flesh on earth. Jesus's Blood has been poured out across all of history and time to reconcile the world back to God. When we mix His Blood with the words of our own testimony (His powerful move in our lives), an unstoppable force is released to those around us. We can overcome all obstacles and encourage the faith of others when we profess the goodness of God through the Blood of Jesus Christ.

@Public

To do something and expect nothing shows a lack of belief.

The only way to defeat the worry is to soak up the Word.

Dishonoring people will have exceedingly negative results in your life. If you want blessings, honor the people around you (Gen.12.3).

Ignore the small, petty fights around you, and you'll have much more time to work towards the bigger, life-changing goals God has for you!

Reading is not just for pleasure; it is for learning and growing. Jesus taught through both fiction and nonfiction. Make time to read!

Perfection is exhausting and honestly impossible. So I'll just stick with excellence.

I'm thankful that I can sit down, open my Bible and read some never-changing truth in a world that can be hectic and chaotic at times.

What people think about you has more to do with what they think of themselves. Hurt souls spread hurting. Healed souls spread healing.

> TO LEARN SOMETHING NEW YOU HAVE TO INVEST A LOT OF TIME AND REALIZE THAT EACH MISTAKE GETS YOU CLOSER TO YOUR GOAL.

A thankful heart may not come naturally, but it can definitely be cultivated. A thankful heart will change your life.

One of many things I admire about Jesus is that He didn't change His tune depending on who was in front of Him. All the "nobodies" and "somebodies" were equally valuable to Him.

If your thoughts are negative and absent of God's joy and peace, start a daily mind workout, capturing every thought and transforming them!

No matter how strict you are on yourself, the enemy will always find ways to shame you. Don't let the devil have that stronghold.

The fear of what people think is more damaging than what they actually do think. People's opinions don't have to affect us one bit.

When we unload the opinions of others that we carry around and worry about, we will more fully enjoy the blessings that God has for us.

When Peter declared that Jesus was the Messiah, Jesus declared Peter was the rock of the Church. When we declare Jesus, He will declare us.

The disciples donated their 7 small loaves to Jesus' work, and He gave them 7 baskets full of loaves back. God will multiply your offerings.

Without a mediator, we stand condemned in our sins and separated from God. But through Jesus we have righteousness and intimacy with God.

Jesus wondered when He comes back to earth, will He find faith? What are we believing in and hoping for today? That is faith and it is good.

You choose your own day! Victory and defeat are choices that aren't dependent on anyone or anything but what you decide for yourself.

God creates lack in your life because He intends to fill it. So find the deep crevices of need and watch how God pours out His abundance!

On the other end of your obedient suffering is a new level of God's glory. Endure patiently and watch God do amazing things in your life.

We shouldn't hoard the platform that God has given us, but rather prayerfully use it to raise other leaders to take more ground for Christ.

Poor advisors will just tell you what you want to hear, but a true friend will lovingly step on your pride to be honest.

The enemy can predict our actions if we work in the flesh. So let's be spontaneous and rely completely on God's mighty work in our spirit!

Your hunger to do God's work should never overshadow your hunger for intimacy with God.

It's hard to heal. It's painful to allow God to touch the broken areas of our lives, but our wounds stay open and infected until He does.

Having the ability to do something, doesn't mean we should do it. Not having the ability to do something, doesn't mean we can't learn how.

God has us wait on our dreams until we believe them based on God's word alone and not on the affirmation of others. Faith is belief.

When God's promises come true in your life may you be so rooted in Him that your character and faith are not easily threatened or enticed.

There is no such thing as a complete failure in God's kingdom if we consistently seek Him!

So many people want to be blessed, but they don't want or can't handle the burdens that come with those blessings. Stewardship takes work.

Jesus loved, healed and saved people, but He also offended them, made them uncomfortable and confronted them. True love goes both ways.

I don't always love reading stories with dramatic irony in them, but I definitely enjoy writing them! Almost done with my 13th book!

Finished my fourth set of edits to Mark within Salvation. Only five more to go! It is so amazing how all the editors bring in their own insights and corrections!

Writing a book is like having a baby. You forget how much blood, sweat and tears it takes from you until you have to push another one out!

I love that Paul doesn't simply say, "a slave of God." No, he says, "a slave of Christ Jesus." God in the flesh, the redemption Person of the Trinity.

> " WHEN PEOPLE READ YOUR BOOK, IT HONESTLY FEELS LIKE THEY ARE READING A PORTION OF YOUR SOUL. "

I love writing my Acknowledgment Page! It's where I get to thank all of my amazing editors. I am so grateful!!!!

Keep the faith! "In the same way, good deeds are obvious, and even those that are not obvious cannot remain hidden forever" (1 Tim 5.25).

Jesus was a Christian fiction "writer" because He spoke the Truth in parables, so we Christian writers are in good Company.

Writer Problems: I feel like I have to clean the house, organize my daughter's closet and plan for the next week before I can start writing.

First time I get to write on my WIP all week. I better get to work and bang out some chapters before mom and wife duties take over!

Teaching long division is as fun as going to the dentist.

Thank God for husbands who help with the kids over the weekend, so you can write. I'm now on chapter 36 with over 70,000 words my WIP.

I enjoy cooking because, unlike writing books, the results are almost immediate.

When God calls me to start something new: "Do not despise these small beginnings, for the Lord rejoices to see the work begin" (Zech. 4.10).

Do something for 30 days that will greatly affect the happiness of your future self, and I promise she will thank you for it.

It's always fun when you find a plot hole in your WIP, and you have to go back through the chapters to fix it.

My husband took our kids out for a fun Saturday afternoon, so I could get some writing done. Yes, he's a keeper and writer's dream spouse.

It's hilarious when you run back to the computer to see what happens next in your book, but then you realize that you still have to write it.

I wrote my 12th chapter (2,000 words) in one hour. Wow! If I keep this up, I'll be done with my book in 30 hours! I just need to find them!

Only chance to write on my book started at 9pm, so I thought I would just write an hour. I look at the clock and it's almost 3 hours later!

Esther invited the king to dine with her and her enemy. When someone's attacking you, always invite the King to join. He will fight for you!

God's teaching you to be a guardian of your promise, not simply a hired hand. That way when the wolves come, you won't abandon your calling.

You will please God when you act according to His promises for your life and not according to how people see you. We please Him by faith.

Don't condemn yourself and your health, peace and joy will escalate! "There is now no condemnation for those who are in Christ Jesus" (Rom. 8.1).

I love when I dream of specific Bible verses that I have to look up when I awake. Recently, I dreamed of Psalm 105.

Hold onto faith especially when nothing is happening. Your hope-fulfilled is just around the corner from your firm belief.

You think the enemy would realize that every time he attacks my mind, I lean deeper into the Lord, His Word and His anointing.

I'm done writing nonfiction! Now I'm switching gears to my next Christian Fiction novel, Mark within Salvation, Book 3 of the Onoma Series!

I got to write almost 4,000 words on my novel today! I love when my characters say profound words and do amazing feats! Makes life fun!

Song of Solomon is truly one of my favorite books in the Bible. Godly passion that is pure, innocent and completely opposite of the world.

It's not legalism; it's love: "If you love me, keep my commands" (John 14.15).

Don't let people or entities brand you with their identity. You have unique value and purpose in Christ that enhances others, not copies.

> A SPIRITUAL GIFT FROM GOD IS EXACTLY THAT: A GIFT. YOU WILL NEVER BE ABLE TO DESERVE OR EARN IT.

It doesn't matter how good it sounds and if everyone agrees with it. If it is not the will of God, it will not prosper or be blessable.

Time flies by when you're writing fiction. I think because you're in another moment, trying your best to see and feel each detail clearly.

As a writer, when one of your characters says or does something that surprises you, you know your readers will be surprised, as well.

We are a discouraged nation because we have lost our vision. We need more prophetic people exhorting and encouraging the Body of Christ.

I finished chapter 1 today of Mark within Salvation, the third book in the Onoma Series! I have a feeling that I will finish fast!

God has really big plans for your life if the foundation is taking so long to build. Be patient with the process. Hold tight to the promise.

Combat every single word of condemnation from the enemy with words of truth from the Bible. In Jesus, you are righteous, holy and loved!

Priorities always get done. If you're struggling with reading the Word, praying, spending time with family, exercising—make it a priority.

Don't always be the rescuer of the relationships you love or else they will grow lopsided. Love enough to expect greatness from others.

Having a firm knowledge of just how much God truly loves you will filter out the negative emotions that fight for position in your mind.

Starve your mind of negative thoughts of worry, anxiety and fear, and give the Holy Spirit room to fill the emptiness with His peace and joy.

People can only give to others what they truly have in themselves—love, encouragement, grace, mercy, wisdom, acceptance, favor and peace.

Treating people like family allows you to love them even when you disagree. We need more mothers, fathers, sisters and brothers in the Church.

It is better to take the time and effort to deal with a problem instead of dragging it into each new day. Ask God to help you work it out.

Our entire worldview changes when we fully grasp the truth that we are loved by Christ. This truth will set us free from our prison of lies.

When your breakthrough comes and God rains down His blessings, you want to be surrounded by the seeds of faith you tenaciously planted.

A quote from my next book, Following God Across the Page: "Sometimes our greatest hopes can become our most difficult burdens."

We must always be moving deeper in our anointing, so we don't try to manufacture yesterday's revelation in today's appointment.

> BE PATIENT. DON'T TAKE SOMETHING IN YOUR STRENGTH THAT GOD WANTS TO GIVE YOU IN HIS STRENGTH.

God will ask me to do something. In my ignorance I obey. Then I discover how hard it is. I stretch in the process. I'm stronger at the end.

You must first be bad at something before you can be good at it. Don't let perfectionism steal your destiny. Start in your weakness today!

That little thing that God wants you to do may seem insignificant, but you don't know how profoundly it will affect someone's life and faith.

Glossing over areas that are in direct contradiction to God's Word deepens strongholds and prevents healing and freedom. Grace needs truth.

Emotional healing, wellness and abundance are tied to Jesus.

Never mistake a person's charisma for God's Spirit. Charisma makes people feel good, but God's Spirit changes lives.

After writing so many books over the years, my mind automatically begins to format information into book form before I even begin writing.

It takes faith to step out on God's promises when all the circumstances around you seem hopeless. Take heart, trust God and move forward!

God can easily change our circumstances, but it's our heart that He wants. Let Him change the inner you and the outer situation will follow.

Become the breakthrough that you've been praying for. If your circumstances don't change, ask God for a change in you. That's the catalyst.

Welcome to the WAIT where God grows your FAITH.

Micromanaging will turn off the creativity of those around us and severely limit our sphere of influence.

So many corporate Christian leaders are trying to dictate to people, but very few spiritual "mothers" and "fathers" are actually investing in people.

Sometimes I wish that life was always fair, but it is through adversity that heroes are born.

Instead of giving up, let's always proclaim: "Perhaps the LORD will act in our behalf. Nothing can hinder the LORD from saving" (1 Sam. 14.6).

Human strategies are meaningless if they are not following God's movements and directives.

Our anointing within us should be continually renewed by God's Spirit to ensure we don't become "settled on our dregs" (Jer. 48.11-12).

I pray that we all gain a greater heavenly perspective of what is pleasing to God and profitable and blessable in His Kingdom on earth.

Your faith will move you towards your promises. Your lack of faith will keep you stagnant.

Cut yourself free from how the world sees you, and you'll be able to enjoy how God sees you: blessed, favored, loved, valued and significant.

When people use their anointing selfishly, it is an inheritance from the Lord that will eventually run out and leave them in the pigpen.

God wants to pull out of you what you're waiting on someone else to do. You are the resource, ability and answer. But you have to rise to it!

Victories are nice, but as you walk with God, they no longer have the authority to define you because God has already named you victorious.

I just read research that found our most creative thoughts come when we're tired. So I guess daylight saving is a good thing for writers???

Don't waste your energy on petty worries and thoughts. Only allow thoughts that have purpose and value to take your time and effort.

I'm writing a book in two weeks, and I have a week and two days left. When God says go, you better hang on!

God's salvation must protect the mind and His righteousness the heart. When you're honest before the Lord, both will be attacked.

Don't let your life be shaped by the definition people try to assign you. Seek the vision God has for you, and find your best self and life.

We must learn to distinguish between our hearts condemning us and the Holy Spirit convicting us. One leads to shame and the other to mercy.

You know the novel you're writing is getting good when you sneak away after dinner to continue writing.

Sometimes we sabotage the very dreams that God has given us because the hope of something lost is easier than the hope of something gained.

POUR YOURSELF INTO YOUR PASSIONS, NOT OTHER PEOPLE'S EXPECTATIONS.

I wrote an entire book in my mind while blow drying my hair! Now I have another writing project to add to my ever growing list.

One of the most difficult things to commit to is making a great idea turn into a reality by diligently accomplishing each detail involved!

If God's promises are like seeds, they will be buried and broken in the supernatural until they sprout in the natural. Water them by faith!

When we help others to prosper, we automatically promote our own prosperity. A house divided falls, but a house unified stands strong.

Many people can sing, write, teach, lead, etc., but very few people can do those things under the anointing of God, igniting transformation.

Sometimes God gives you rest, but other times He wants you to dig into the Word as much as you can because He's preparing you for something!

Trying to better oneself is very difficult without a deep sense of being loved and valued and full of purpose and meaning.

Falling out of devotion with the Lord is a gradual decline, but it only takes an instant for God to set you back up in fellowship with Him.

Just wondering if the Golden Rule, "Love God and love others as yourself" is apparent on our social media sites.

We can go quite a ways in our own limited strength, but when we rely on God's unlimited strength, our journey with Him is limitless!

Sometimes God cuts all your attachments because He's about to move you into a new direction and place you on a higher plane.

If you are struggling right now, there is a victory on the other side, which is ALWAYS more blessing, revelation and intimacy with Jesus.

Being a victim all the time can be a form of pride because you never have to take responsibility for your choices, actions and circumstances.

God's love is more powerful than human protocol, and His mercy more meaningful than human effort. Resting in God's grace changes everything.

Our soul becomes "greatly worn out and distressed" when we stay in a dark place for too long, but God can rescue us (2 Peter 2.7 AMP).

If Jesus says it is possible and your circumstances say it is impossible, trust His Word and apply your faith. God's will usurps everything!

Sometimes walking with God feels like a slow uphill climb. Other times it takes all your energy just to keep up.

Our influence resides in our anointing. Find your purpose and you'll feel God's power rise up within you.

A sentence from my new book: Grace allows us to be aware of both our weaknesses and strengths, yet still feel secure in who we are in Christ.

Our fear of something gives it power. Replace your fear with faith, and its control over you will dissolve.

To believe that Christians should all be perfect is ironic because it is our imperfections that cause us to reach for Jesus.

Only when you believe in yourself can you fully believe in others! God says you are worthy, loved, valued and full of purpose!

Rather than focus on our sin, we can focus on how much Jesus loves us. God's correction works way better than our condemnation.

> IT'S FRUITLESS TO CONSIDER ALL YOUR OPTIONS UNTIL YOU FIRST GO TO GOD IN PRAYER.

We struggle with new responsibilities because at first they feel hard. But if we keep at them, we will grow stronger until they feel easy.

Need some of God's power in your life today? "Lord, there is no one like you! For you are great, and your NAME is full of POWER" (Jeremiah 10.6).

It's hard to hold grudges against people when you're surrounded by God's blessings and grace. Sometimes we just need to remind ourselves.

@Private

My platform will be like a baby. God has so much glory that He needs to establish on earth, but few people are willing to take it. His glory divides people. They may hate and torment me, but others will understand the circumstances. Lord, I give You this baby, this platform, that has not yet been established. I will not regret Your promises in my life. I will not allow them to change my family. God is doing something new in me, and I will feel the bites of haters. But I choose to rise above the noise and chaos. I will not take my fire-hydrant platform for granted. Go with me, Lord. Be my upper and lower springs. I am perfect, holy and beautiful in Your eyes through Jesus Christ. I love You, Lord. Transform my life. Give me purpose. Thunder through me. You are my Father, and I am cherished!

Immediately, after Jesus fed the 5,000 miraculously, He made the disciples leave—not to get too filled up with praise? Jesus made the disciples get into the boat and go ahead of Him into a difficult storm. Command me, Lord, to come to You! Force my eyes to stay on You. The storm stopped when Jesus got into the boat. Teach me how to reach for You. Teach me how to teach others how to reach Jesus. God will bring us to a place where only He can provide. If we seek human help, it will do nothing but hinder God's move.

Leaders in Christ are fully supplied both naturally and supernaturally. I have come before God's throne, and He has dismissed all charges against me. My breakthrough will come, and I will achieve my destiny that has been written in books before I was born. I accept the resurrection power in my life. I am Jesus' sister, and God is our Father. I will walk in confidence because my royalty will never fade. I am free. I am confident. I am worthy. I am loved. I am valued. I have a large platform. I receive one grace after another, one spiritual blessing after another and one favor after another.

I know who I am in Christ. I am a vessel of mercy. I am loved and I feel His pleasure. I won't be bullied by stupid imaginings anymore. Breakthrough in me, Lord. I want to be the best wife and mother. Let me pour into my family. I have no condemnation in Christ. God has an amazing platform for me according to His promises. I am an apostolic mother to many voices. I break the religious spirit in my life. God will use me for His mighty purpose and pour His abundance through me!

Forgive me for judging Your children. Manifest in the natural what is all around me in the spiritual. I am a royal daughter and I have great authority. I have a huge Promised Land. I have abundant fruit. Rewire my brain to be eternally minded. Renew my mind, heart and spirit. Protect my kids and allow them to roar. Guide me on ancient paths. I want my mind to be a springboard for God's glory. I have written fourteen books. I will reach people for Christ. My writing is lethal to the enemy—by the Blood of the Lamb and the words of our testimony (Revelation 12.11)!

#YEAR 8

"For this is what the LORD, the God of Israel, says: There will always be flour and olive oil left in your containers until the time when the Lord sends rain and the crops grow again!" (1 Kings 17.14 NLT).

Waiting on God to send His rain upon our harvest of obedience reveals our faith. If we truly believe God at His Word, nothing will cause us to walk away from His promises—even when all feels dead and lost. As we wait, though, God says that He will provide for us. He will give us exactly what we need each day to continue on our journey of faith. Yes, the promises may yet linger, but that doesn't mean God has abandoned us. We can continue to cultivate a deeper relationship with God as He cares for us each day. Our intimacy with the Lord is what will ground us when the rains of promise are finally released.

@Public

God's promises look different for everyone.

Any habits in your life that are not God's best can be transformed into something beneficial with a little ingenuity and willpower!

If you are feeling low, Jesus will lift you up! If you are broken, He will heal you! If you are stressed, He will give you peace!

Just work on the page that is in front of you, trusting that God will unfold the entire story through your faithfulness in His time.

If we only focus on the negative in people, the good in them will eventually fade in our eyes until all we see is ugliness.

Ignore small minded, petty people who like to nip at others. Don't sink to their level; instead, continue on the journey of the highroad.

Capture and destroy every thought and word that opposes God's good plan for your life!

We must know and embrace our worth in Christ, so we can make decisions and actions based on our belief in that worth.

The word "repent" means to go back and to rise again. Rise to the truth that you are God's righteousness through the Finished Work of Jesus.

If we believe Jesus for forgiveness, we must also believe Him for righteousness. Jesus took our mistakes and replaced them with His perfection.

I love writing about Jesus because He is relevant in every single area of our lives. There is nothing that He cannot touch and transform!

Often, God puts us around people who have what we want, not to shame us but to show us what is possible when we trust in Him.

Many things aren't necessarily bad or wrong; they just fall short of God's best.

Sometimes you have to speak to that void in your life by faith. We have God's creative ability to create greatness out of our emptiness.

> WHATEVER YOU NEED GOD HAS IT READY TO GIVE YOU, BUT YOU MUST BELIEVE TO RECEIVE.

God will give us the answers that we need when we quit trying to do everything in our own strength. Stop. Look. Listen. Wait.

Working in our own strength may produce instant fruit, but when we wait on the Lord, the fruit He produces will be powerful and limitless.

I would rather take the highroad than get caught in the middle of mudslinging. I love America and Americans even though we aren't perfect.

Using the excuse of "I don't know how," is not a reason to disobey a direct order from God. Have faith and learn how to do it.

We would be so pleased with the gifts and blessings God has given each of us personally if we didn't compare ourselves and lives to others.

God's best is the hardest reality to achieve because we are swamped in our sinful state, but if we follow the Holy Spirit, we will make it!

Don't put anyone on a pedestal except Jesus. He is the only one who deserves our worship.

So often following after Jesus will lead us into a place of lack and need, but that is when Jesus manifests His best miracles in our lives.

Editing nonfiction is never as fun as editing fiction. Can't wait to write another fiction book, so I can get wrapped up in the story!

Often God's promises to you will have to die, so He can resurrect them in His power. We must cling onto faith even when our dreams seem dead.

We've all been on the two sides of hurt—both receiving and afflicting it. Life is messy, which is why we must cling onto God's mercy.

I have to read God's Word and other devotionals until I feel God's victory for my day rise up. Some days, like today, take a lot of reading.

It is so much easier to focus on doing God's will rather than trying to be perfect all the time.

Let us never use our service to God as an excuse to ignore the needs of the people right in front of us.

Much of our stress would be eliminated if we just gave our expectations to God.

I did a ton of writing today. It never fails that when I commit to working in my calling as a writer that I feel so energized afterward!

Drastic changes aren't always necessary to achieving our dreams. Many times the small, simple changes in life will make all the difference.

If you're carrying around guilt you have to ask yourself this one question: What's more powerful? Your mistakes or His blood?

Don't compare your life story to others. God's imagination is endless. He'll get you to your victory on a different path and in a new way.

Focus on consuming more water and you will automatically consume less soda. Consume more of God and you will consume less of the world.

The difference between spiritual confidence and spiritual pride is that one is rooted in Jesus and the other is rooted in self.

Unhealed physical wounds leave your body open to disease, decay and even death...same is true for spiritual wounds and your spiritual body.

Sometimes we are so focused on the Hands of God (His Work) that we forget about the Heart of God (His Love). Love must always precede work.

Sometimes God withholds His healing, His breakthrough and His promise for a season because He's going to teach and grow you in the struggle.

If God has given you a promise; say it, claim it and believe it every moment of every day until it comes to pass! Do not let doubt set in!

It's easy to write to the applause of the crowd, but it takes determination to write to the silence of the desert.

God will allow our lives to become uncomfortable, so we can finally reach out for Jesus. He is our only hope for an eternal place with God.

> " THERE IS MORE POWER IN YOUR SECRET INTIMACY WITH THE LORD THAN THERE IS IN ALL YOUR GOOD WORKS DONE BEFORE OTHERS. "

We must turn our criticism of others into intercession for others, so we can release the grace, mercy and blessing of God into our lives.

Be who God designed and destined you to be. Your life will not be easy, but at least you'll never have to question your purpose.

We can look beyond our own hurts and pains to see the bigger picture of what God is accomplishing through us and our circumstances.

If people lie about you and speak evil over you, don't worry. You are in good company. They did that to Jesus, but he had the final victory.

It's awesome when you truly believe that you don't need anyone else's approval besides God's!

It's absurd to think you can speak sweetly to a man while stabbing his wife in the back. When the wife is attacked, a godly man feels it.

We can't lie and cheat, acquiring ill-gotten gain and expect to keep it. We reap what we sow. Lies and cheats will be eventually exposed.

Some people will have pushed everyone in their life away before they finally realize that they were the problem.

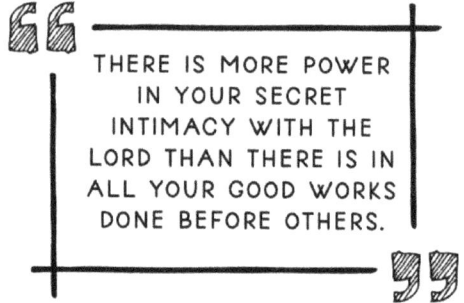

We can be aggressive about replacing ugly things in our life with something beautiful. And replacing what has been lost with what's found.

Our worldview will change if we walk in the truth that we are victors through Christ, not victims! Words, actions and deeds will transform!

Run from people who ignore and cover up your good qualities, so they can spend their time highlighting and exaggerating your flaws!

The haters and deceivers in your life reveal themselves quickly when the storm hits. Take note, shake off the dust and move on.

Lots of writing accomplished yesterday and today. Hoping the rest of the week will be just as productive!

When people easily throw something away (job, relationship, idea, etc.), it's a sure sign that they were never fully committed and invested.

The world is falling apart and Christians are so distracted with their personal drama that they can't engage in the larger battle around us.

Sometimes God allows the true colors of people to come out not to hurt you, but to reveal how ugly their hearts are toward you. Take heed!

Instantly rebuke every word that is spoken over you that isn't rooted in love and truth. Don't agonize over lies. They don't belong to you!

Don't let the approval of others dictate your purpose. Trust God and the desires He has given you and run your race to win!

Be still in the chaos and God will redeem you. Be quiet in the storm and God will protect you. Be firm against all odds and watch God work!

Choose to turn your FEAR into FAITH, and I promise that you will have a better day even in the SAME circumstances!!

God can use your struggle to bring people closer to Him, as they watch you cling onto hope in Jesus even during the darkest of times.

Jesus is the manifestation of the power and the will of God on earth and in our lives. If you want to know God, you must begin with Christ.

Don't allow the great things that God is doing in the lives of others to diminish the great things He is doing in your own life.

The leading figures in the Bible who achieved great victories ALL had to freely accept mercy or they could have never been used so mightily.

Maintaining perseverance along with receiving mercy ensures our victory! Without mercy we'll fall into legalism, which fosters deception.

When life gets hard, I'm reminded how blessed I am that God has built me to handle it. I pray for strength to do more, give more, live more!

God makes a supernatural joy and peace available to us every moment. Let us not allow anything to hinder us from claiming and grasping them.

We must daily guard our faith in God's Word and His promises because that is the main area the enemy wants to destroy.

People want to do more for those who have a grateful heart. But a heart set on selfishness and criticism will push blessings and gifts away.

God sees your misery, and He wants to end your suffering. Work with Him to get out of your bondage. The pain of change is worth being free.

In certain situations and with a few specific individuals, it's best to take Jesus' advice: "Ignore them. They are blind..." (Matt. 15.14).

> IF YOU DON'T LET THE WORLD CHANGE YOU, GOD WILL USE YOU TO CHANGE THE WORLD.

No matter where you are in life and how far you've gone down the same path, you can ALWAYS change course! A new route only takes one step!

I'd rather be a product of obedience than a product of circumstance.

Some people have to imagine a monster in others, so they can avoid the monster in themselves. "Search me, O God, and know my heart" (Psalm 139.23).

Never lower yourself to fit someone else's insecurities. Walk in the freedom of God's opinion of you.

When God doesn't give you a supernatural breakthrough in your situation, ask Him to unleash a supernatural breakthrough in your spirit.

It is difficult becoming someone we are not, but if God sees it in us, we have to believe that we will eventually get there!

Negative self-talk is an emotional form of self-injury. Every ugly word is like a slash on our arm. We must decide to change our words!

Forgiveness doesn't mean we sweep chronic issues under the rug. It means we give God the hurt while we deal with the root of the problem.

Great word from the Lord today that I read in my book, Slay the Day. When God calls us to do the "paperwork" of life, we should obey!

When you settle your heart on how God sees you and how much He loves you, you will be released from the destructive opinions of others.

It's okay to be angry, but we must try not to sin in our anger. We can always trust that God will bring grace and truth into all situations!

The easy way is to blame others, so you won't have to change. It takes strength to see your own failures, allowing God to transform you.

Make sure to receive a word from the Lord before starting anything new. That way you won't give up when things get hard because they will.

People who have ignored their own anointing from God will try to twist yours into something ugly. Dismiss their words and walk in purpose!

If we do not allow God to heal our wounds, we can become like venomous snakes, biting and poisoning the people around us, especially family.

If someone speaks evil words over you, declaring what the devil wants you to think about yourself, rebuke the words right away in Jesus!

We can honor others without honoring their abusive actions towards us by setting up healthy boundaries.

It takes double the time getting warmed up to write than the actual time needed to write.

If Jesus can command us to love our neighbors as ourselves, then love is a choice not a feeling. Love doesn't have to feel good to be right.

Maybe if I had readers surrounding me, encouraging me to keep writing, I would stop getting so distracted! I know God is rooting me on!

Being in an actual MMA bout myself makes writing about Paul's words about boxing and fighting so much more engaging because I've been there!

Your followers and worldly influence say nothing about who you are bringing to heaven with you. That is the ONLY thing that matters in life!

So many of us want to change the world, but if we are not firm in the Lord, the world will eventually change us. Take courage! Stand firm!

We can focus on all the little things we do wrong or on all the BIG things God does right! God will ALWAYS be strong in our weakness!

Ignore people who criticize what you are passionate about. If God gave you those passions, He will use them to shine His glory!

Remember when we had to occupy our time with our thoughts and not with our phones? Turning mine off for the evening.

Wait on God's timing. Stay faithful to His calling. And He will bring down the former and the latter rains onto your promises!!

Your struggles lead to your strengths. Don't avoid the difficulties in life. Run after them with both fists ready for the fight!

I'm becoming a formatting genius! I just learned how to add and delete section breaks in a book. Every roadblock causes me to learn more!

When we have a firm understanding of what God has called us to do, the waiting for harvest won't cause us to stumble and give up.

Submitted my book for review today. It's interesting that every time I publish a book, I learn something new. I'm always growing as a writer.

We can no longer doubt God's promises. It's not about "IF" but "WHEN." He will fulfill His plans for your life, and the rains will unleash!

It's a shame to labor for something with no eternal value. Our good works may seem pleasing to the world, but they must be rooted in Christ.

> **DON'T LET INSECURITY CAUSE YOU TO DEVALUE OR DISCOUNT GOD'S ANOINTING IN YOUR LIFE. HAVE FAITH IN THE PROMISES THAT HE HAS SPOKEN OVER YOU!**

Our actions will ALWAYS be in direct relation to our thoughts. So what are we thinking today? Thoughts of hope or thoughts of despair?

Our biggest struggle is usually not our circumstances, but our thoughts. We can choose to focus on our fear and doubt or our faith and belief.

It's easy to slip into petty frustrations when we lose our focus on eternity. When we keep our eyes on Jesus, the small things disappear.

If we so desperately want to be the victim in every situation, we will never be the victor. God has called us and assigned us to overcome!

It's an amazing moment when you start doing what you're called to do because you WANT to and not because you HAVE to!!!

Sin covered up is a disease eating away at the soul, but sin revealed is a salvation salve for the body, mind and spirit!

Seek the best in people even when they seek the worst in you, trusting that God will always redeem those He loves with His grace and favor.

Many of our body's problems would go away if we drank more water. And many of our life's problems would go away If we drank more Bible.

The Lord leads you into the desert promising you springs; and when you feel the dryness, you must believe He'll create a stream in the sand.

I wonder how long John the Baptist talked to an empty field until the crowds started showing up. Stay faithful even when no one's listening.

Don't lose hope! God will give you enough flour and oil to sustain you while you wait for Him to send the rains in your life! (1 Kings 17).

Switching gears from nonfiction to fiction: two paths of writing that go in opposite directions, but I can do this!

When I finally get a chance to sit down and write, I write as fast and as much as I can because life's responsibilities always beckon!

I love when I listen to God when He says to wait and a short time later He provides even more than what I needed without all the fuss.

The first chapter of every book is the hardest to write! You just have to sit down, start clicking at the keyboard and pray the words come.

If we were more concerned about how God sees us vs. how the world sees us, we would be in a much better place emotionally and spiritually.

Don't give up on people midway through the process that God is putting them through. They will eventually surprise you, so don't miss out.

> **WE MUST TAKE CARE NOT TO WALK A ROAD TO DESTRUCTION PAVED WITH "GOOD WORKS" THAT DEFY THE WILL OF GOD AND HIS PURPOSES FOR OUR LIVES.**

@Private

I'm ready for a revelation! I have not been anointed by people but by God Himself. I don't need promotion from people. I have an apostolic appointment from God. I will ignite a fire in my church, my community and nation. I will pour into my readers! I pray they understand the power of their words and allow my books to change them.

I feel so knocked down. My promises from God are so dead, and my writing ministry is a dry desert. Every time I muster up my strength and gather my faith, the enemy of my soul and purpose knocks me over. I feel like I'm at my lowest. There seems to be nothing redeemable about me. It feels like God has found me unfit and unworthy to carry His promises for my life. My books are stagnant and lifeless, yet I must continue to write. Every book is stillborn. What am I to do? I understand that God is strong in my stupid, corruptible weakness. I have fruit in my marriage and with my kids, but the desert of my promises is encroaching into my home, trying to dry out my entire life. It feels like I need to cut the dead areas of my life, which is my writing.

I had a dream that I was in a desolate town and in this impoverished house. We had to live there for some reason. The steward of the house said this was all there was. I looked at all the bedrooms and the beds were made of cement with no covers. I said my kids can't live like this. So the woman said that I would have to build a hotel. I said okay, but when I stepped outside, I was so surprised! Just up a large, grassy hill full of trees. I saw condos, hotels and resorts. It was lush and beautiful. I thought to myself that I will not have to build my own hotel. I would take my family up the hill and stay at the resort.

The woman had tried to deceive me by telling me there was no other place to stay. The enemy will try to tell us that we have to build our own platform in our lack, but God has resorts already prepared for us if we labor unto His rest! I have forsaken building my own platform. I have been laboring up that hill with my family to rest in the abundance God already has for me.

───────────

No one is buying my books. I might sell five a month. I don't know how to get people to buy them. I just have to keep writing and ignore the numbers. I wonder how long John the Baptist preached to empty fields before the crowds came? Lord, make Your mark on me. Let me be in tune with You that I barely struggle with doing the right thing. Pick me up, Lord. I struggle with doubt and insecurity. I want all of my hope and confidence to be in Jesus.

#YEAR 7

"And so, Lord, where do I put my hope? My only hope is in you"
(Psalm 39.7 NLT).

It can be tempting to put our hope into people and circumstances—
anything that doesn't take faith. Our anticipation may get a
momentary boost when we think something tangible is going to fulfill
our dreams for us, but true faith is rooted in the unseen. Although God
can use people and situations to complete His agenda, our faith should
rely on His Word alone and not human help. God is all-powerful, and if
He finds no one to accomplish His will, He will wield His mighty hand to
bring His plans to fruition. Many times, He will take away all earthly
help in order to produce faith in us. He wants to ensure that we
believe simply because He says so.

@Public

We don't have to jump around looking for God-inspired movements
because we ourselves can be a well-spring of God's glory to the world!

If you glorify God in all that you do, you will transform mundane, everyday tasks into the highest calling known to all of creation.

May we be so rooted in Christ that we move as one with the Holy Spirit. May our very lives be an outpouring of God's presence to the world.

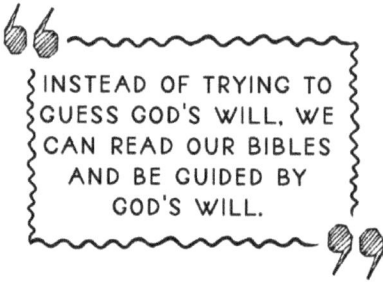

> INSTEAD OF TRYING TO GUESS GOD'S WILL, WE CAN READ OUR BIBLES AND BE GUIDED BY GOD'S WILL.

After more edits, I finally submitted my Bear into Redemption book files. I should receive my proof soon and publish my book by Christmas!

It's always a fun day when you spend hours formatting each paragraph in a 400 page book only to have to undo every single thing you changed.

Those who try to push God's promises to a quick fulfillment will not experience the supernatural power and awesomeness of what God can do.

I'm thankful that I can be me and fully embrace the design that God gave me. Only then can I truly fulfill all that God has planned for me.

My husband is almost done reading my next novel, Bear into Redemption! That last 10 chapters will be hard for him to put down!

Truth is that we will disappoint people and they will disappoint us, which is why we need to learn to both give and receive grace.

It's so easy for people to think they can do a better job when they are all words and no action!

I finished my edits for Bear into Redemption and sent it to a group of amazing readers (friends/family) who will be giving me their insight!

It's awesome to read your newly finished novel as a reader and not a writer. I already know what happens, but I'm still enthralled!

If we seek validation from others, we will be let down. But if we seek validation from God through Jesus, even our mistakes cannot shame us.

Negative people will come out of the woodwork when you are doing God's will. Apathetic people don't like seeing others being used by God.

Give your best in every situation no matter the apathy of those around you. The difference between you and them will eventually show.

> **WE SHOW BELIEF IN GOD'S PROMISES FOR OUR LIVES WHEN WE ARE WILLING TO SUFFER FOR THEM.**

Sometimes we are so occupied with the outside world that we forget that God is trying to produce something great within us.

Don't be discouraged when God isolates you. Both Newton and Einstein made their greatest discoveries when they were cut off from others.

All my neighbors stopped to help me with my mischievous, stubborn but completely adorable dachshund who decided to chase my sister's car!

My husband is so amazing! He is taking the kids for the next several hours so I can finish a bunch of edits, curriculum and writing!

I'd rather be in a small group of the completely committed than a large group of the half-hearted.

Our hope should be in the Lord and not people. He alone can fulfill His promises to us. He can use people, but He has to move their hearts.

Editing my novel after it's finally been written is my absolute favorite part of writing. I'm ready to make my story even better!

I'm done with the first draft of Bear into Redemption! 42 chapters and 96,000 words. I am so unbelievably happy! Now time for the editing!

My prayer for years was for God to give me more time to write, but instead of diminishing my Kingdom influence, He made me a faster writer!

I'm writing curriculum for this week's Christian Imagination class. We will discuss the importance of the opening line to a work of fiction.

Done with chapter 31 of Bear into Redemption! I love my characters. They are always surprising me and showing me their humanity!

Why does the act of writing have to be so sedentary???

I had to rewrite chapter 29 and add another scene, but it is done. Now it is time to write the climax of this book and finished this draft!

I wasn't inspired to write on my novel today, so I wrote a children's book instead. It looks like my genre repertoire is expanding again!

Sometimes God's favor shows up in closed doors, but we don't see it until many years later. Thank You, Lord, for every "NO" I have received!

I know there are two more hours left in the day, but there is no way I can write another single word. Tired and ready to relax my brain!

I love when my kids ask me faith questions. I usually have an answer, not an answer of knowledge, but an answer revealed by the Holy Spirit.

My spirit is restless. I'm praying for all those who need protection and comfort today. May God continue to care and watch over you.

Is it wrong to applaud after you finish writing the most awesome chapter ever!!! I love how the story just unfolds, and I try to keep up!

When we remember that God has sent us on the journey, the difficult steps along the way won't cause us to quit. The victory is the Lord's!

It's such a pain to move computers when you're a writer. So many software products need to be bought and so many files moved.

God cannot expand our sphere of influence if we need to be perfect in everyone's eyes. Eventually, people will find that we need grace too.

If we can create a spirit of worship to God without a crowd, without acclaim, without recognition, we have achieved a faith that few claim.

There is so much power in Jesus' name to claim the desires that God Himself has given us so that our JOY in Him will be complete (John 16.24).

I can finally sit down to write now that the house is picked up, the laundry put away, the dishes washed and the dog walked.

If we are not humbled to the Lord, we won't be empowered by His Spirit. Our own pride minimizes what He can accomplish in our lives.

Looks like I'll be writing another scene, so I think another cup of coffee is in order. Let's do this!

Do not waste your time defending yourself against the ignorant opinions of others. Their own pride has to knock others down to feel better.

I don't make a strict outline when I write my fiction novels. Instead, I get lost in the scenes and dialogue of each character!

No more analyzing, floundering and wondering! It's time to unleash a season of action, discipline and transformation starting today!

Even on our worst day, God is wanting to show us His love. We simply need to perceive it and receive it!

I'm very excited that I got two hours of writing done before the craziness of the day steals all of my hours!

I'd rather offend others than offend God and doing nothing is the biggest offense.

We are called to love people, but we are not called to cater to sin.

Our little steps of obedience are usually portals to a God-designed plan that is way bigger than we could ever imagine!

Our life is not valuable according to the thoughts of people. Our life is valuable according to the thoughts of God!

> RESTING IN THE LORD IS JUST AS IMPORTANT AS WORKING FOR THE LORD.

No matter how dark the atmosphere is around us, we must not be ruled by fear. Instead, we can strengthen our faith in the Lord.

We are taking our kids to a fancy restaurant because life is too short not to get fancy every once in a while!

I will not rely on people to achieve only what God can do.

Both our words and our hearts need to be rooted in God. Otherwise, our Christian talk means nothing and our lives will be eternally empty.

We can use the resources and abilities God has gifted us to refresh the people around us, like David used the harp.

Stay in God's Word and claim His peace! "Great PEACE have those who love Your law, and NOTHING causes them to stumble" (Psalm 119.165).

Done with my book signing! I'm so thankful for everyone's show of support! I pray a blessing of God's favor over the readers of my books!

The atmosphere of our government and society today does not change God, His love for us and our desperate need for Jesus! God is unshakable!

I'm stepping into extrovert mode and getting my social butterfly hat on. My book signing is today, and I'm ready to sign!

Claim your promises not according to your circumstances but according to God's faithfulness today!!!

I know that I'm biased as a writer, but I really do love readers.

I finally understand that when I'm humble to the Lord (not perfect), He will exalt Himself in my life. I just have to be still (Psalm 46.10).

God is awesome at using the circumstances in our lives to teach and mold us. Again I'm reminded to rise above the noise and claim victory!

I just submitted my book, Fearlessly Fit, for the final review! Hopefully, I will be doing a book signing late June! Details to come!

I received my final endorsement for my book, Fearlessly Fit! It will be published next week! Can't wait!!!

> I WANT TO BE A PERSON WHO HAS HER EYES ON WHAT UNITES PEOPLE, NOT WHAT DIVIDES US.

The Lord's hand is powerful, and it moves mightily on behalf of all those who seek His help!

Instead of being wrapped up in a cause, we need to be wrapped up in Christ, and He will make us a cause of great change for His Kingdom!

I am claiming it! I will be done writing the first draft of my 7th book tomorrow. In Jesus' name Amen!

My legs are starting to cramp up from sitting and writing for the past several days :(I need to hurry up and push out this book!

I'm almost done writing my next book, and all I can think about is that I want the color scheme of my cover to include periwinkle.

I got a full day of writing ahead of me. I really want to make a dent in my next book. Excited about shaping thoughts on paper.

Everyone is looking for John-the-Baptist-Faith, but they have to be willing to go to the wilderness to find it.

When you start obeying God on a whole new level, be prepared for a crop of brand-new devils.

Sometimes you have to ignore your emotions and choose to walk in God's Truth and the promises found in His Word.

Super excited!! I am now certified in fitness nutrition. I'm done taking tests for a while. Now it's time to get back to my writing!

I finished reading almost 500 pages of nutrition information, learned too much biochemistry and took my nutrition certificate test. DONE!!!

I have found that the answer to our greatest struggles in life is many times found in our own attitudes.

God allows struggles in our lives to make us stronger. It's not about being a victim; it's about overcoming to become a conqueror.

We need to let go of the "Woe is me" mentality and get into "Wow is me" mode! We have been beautifully made by a God who loves and adores us!

Words are filled with life! We need to be diligent about speaking good, empowering and faith-filled words over people!

One of the hardest things to do as a Christian is to stay obedient to God even when you know someone will be offended, disappointed or hurt.

God gives each of us burdens in this life, but when we stay in contact with Him and rely on His strength, the burdens will be easy to bear!

I've published 5 nonfiction books since January of this year. I'm writing one more, and then it's back to writing fiction for a long while!

Don't put people on a pedestal because they will eventually fall from grace in your eyes, but the truth is they need grace just like you.

God leads us to both victories and failures, as long as we consulted the Holy Spirit first, it doesn't matter which outcome we get.

No matter what you're doing, when you're submitted to God and choose to be in the center of His will, you'll find yourself in complete peace.

Note to self: Never try to format your book late at night when you're dead tired. You'll have to fix all your craziness the next morning.

There are some things that we will only learn through trial and error. We shouldn't be so hard on ourselves when we make mistakes.

We must not always save people from experiencing difficulty because it is the hard times that reveal our absolute need for Christ.

When just one person says that my book has drawn her closer to Jesus, the long hours spent writing and editing seem of little consequence.

Older gentlemen riding his Harley down the highway with his walker securely strapped over his handlebars. Awesomeness!

I was discouraged by how much I have to go to finish my one year devotional that I forgot how much I've already done. Over 61,000 words so far!

Just like Jesus did with the bread, God will bless you, break you and multiply you, so you can be a blessing to others.

Lately, I feel so worn out that I don't think I can write, but God says it's a perfect time to supply me with His power, energy and grace!

I never want to be content with previous victories. I always want to be growing, changing, learning and gaining new ground!

> **THE POWER OF SIN DIED ON THE CROSS, AND THE POWER OF GRACE ROSE FROM THE TOMB! WE HAVE THE VICTORY OVER DEATH THROUGH JESUS CHRIST!**

Our pride is hurt when we are offended, but if our pride is dead, we would only feel the love, worth and acceptance of God through Jesus.

When we allow God to soften and heal our wounds, we are better able to live for Him (Isaiah 1.5-6).

Walk in your anointing by faith before your God-given promises become evident in this world, and you will make all of heaven stand in awe.

The main thing God needs from us is our submission. After that, He will give us the knowledge, resources and abilities to achieve His purpose!

No matter the resources that the world brings to the table, they will never come close to the supernatural power of having God on your side!

I just finished writing my second article. One more to go, and I can take a break and learn something fun.

When God finally releases us to reap a harvest, an awesome thing occurs: not only are we blessed, but God's Children everywhere are blessed.

They will say your words have no value and your life has no worth, and they will try to steal your God-given destiny. But don't fear! Trust God!

I write not for selfish gain but for Kingdom gain! I work not for self-glory but for His glory! My feet are on earth and my eyes on eternity!

It's a special moment when you read your own writing and you see the imprint of the Holy Spirit, pouring out wisdom that is beyond you!

When the luster of newness wears thin, that's when our determination kicks in!

Complacency mocks our God who died to give us free will, so we could exert our creative authority on earth for His glory.

I love this line I wrote: Every weight of difficulty thrown against us during our lives is simply a means of getting us stronger in Christ.

Sometimes I wish that the words I want to write would just fall out of my brain onto pages of a book in grammatical and contextual order.

Pray most of all to have the fear of the Lord, for it saves us from making decisions outside the will of God, which causes turmoil in life.

Jesus died with sin and death. Then He took back up His life and left them in the tomb! We are free from sin because of Jesus' finished work!!!

My prayer for those of us who need direction: "Show me the right path, O LORD; point out the road for me to follow" (Psalm 25:4 NLT).

Life is so much better when we focus on what God is doing in our own lives and not what God is doing in everyone else's life!

Don't get distracted by what well-meaning people tell you to do. Only commit to God's plans for your life, and He will establish your steps!

It is interesting to note that the original Bible in Hebrew and Aramaic was written without punctuation.

People thrive when there is peace in the home. That is why the ministry of marriage and family is so important!

If your negative circumstances are out of your control, you might as well continue to praise God. Words of doubt will only cause more harm.

> WE NEVER HAVE TO APOLOGIZE FOR NOT BEING PERFECT BECAUSE WE NEVER CLAIMED TO BE.

Getting ready to write my first fight scene for my next novel, Bear into Redemption! Super excited. It's going to be epic.

Keep claiming God's promises until they come to pass! Words of life!

When my kids say that they are bored, I tell them that they should be grateful. "Because if you are bored that means you are blessed!"

@Private

You have already told me, Lord, that my writing would be "leaps and stops" vs. a slow jog. Well, I have 2 months to write 2 books, train for a bodybuilding competition and get certified as a personal trainer. Help me, Lord, to work diligently without compromising my relationship with You and my family.

Today, I worked out my legs so hard that my legs are so tight. I will need to run tomorrow to loosen them up. This makes me think of my spiritual growth. I have worked out so hard spiritually that I'm tight with inactivity. I want God to unleash my platform. I want to be used by God, but I also don't want to whine about the platform that He gives me. I want to live in the freedom of grace. God, please prove all the people who devalued Your work in my life wrong. It is not I they are rejecting, but Your anointing and Your authority in me.

———

I am lacking hope. I would be working on my debut novel ten years ago. I would be wrestling with truths that I didn't understand and writing a format that was new to me. My entire obedience would be set on self-glory masked as righteousness. And when I finally finished the book in January 2006, I would begin my long journey of breaking, shaping and faithing. God would reveal layers upon layers of selfishness, replacing them with His design for me. And I would resist Him or fear the process – clenching my teeth and waiting for each blow with anxiety. Until each year that passed would eat away at my faith like cancer. Almost 10 years of waiting and working towards a prize that I have not seen has put me in a state of hopelessness. Will I be like Abraham who still believed or will I laugh like Sarah in disbelief?

I've tried to fill my hopelessness with things of this world, not indulgent but as a band-aid to cover the pain. But I don't need a band-aid. I need a transformation. I need my promises to be resurrected. God has blessed me so much in life. I could walk away from my calling and enjoy my amazing husband, my awesome kids and the lifestyle that God has given me. I would be content if it weren't for God's Promises pressing on my spirit. I have destiny. I am to be a force for God. He has put me through the fires to refine my life like gold. He will use me! But when? It's been ten years, but my hope is in the Lord. Grant me supernatural hope, Lord.

God's promises have never felt so heavy on me. I fight bitterness all through the day, forcing my faith to cling onto hope. God is building something large in me, and I will believe despite the overwhelming desolation of my dreams—not one of my books has sold this month. I will believe that God's promise to have a large platform will come to pass. Lord, today I read that it is okay to ask for a sign. Please, Father, don't forget about me and Your promises for my life. Please don't let another day go by with me waiting. Stand up in my writing. Let everyone know that You are moving mightily in my obedience! Show Yourself to me. I don't want to wait anymore. Ten years is long enough. I will continue to be faithful.

#YEAR 6

"And my message and my preaching were very plain. Rather than using clever and persuasive speeches, I relied only on the power of the Holy Spirit" (1 Corinthians 2.4 NLT).

When we rely on our own strength, intelligence and charisma, we disregard the supernatural power of God's Spirit. Anything we achieve by our own authority, we will have to maintain with that same authority. Eventually, though, we will lose stamina and burn out. Our strength and resources are finite, but God's strength and resources are limitless. As we learn to rely on the power of the Holy Spirit, we begin to rest in His work. Moreover, we will find that God is much more capable than we are at accomplishing His Kingdom Plans. We can yield to His movements and allow Him to establish greater things than we could ever imagine through and in us.

@Public

I am about to publish my first book under my OWN publishing label, Marked Writers Publishing! This is going to be an AMAZING new year!

You know your belief in God is shining through when your decisions and actions make absolutely no sense in the natural!

Our own pride is the culprit for most of our suffering. Only in humility will we find freedom and joy in Christ.

While reading over my nonfiction book, I'm noticing a lot of fiction elements in my writing. I guess I can't get away from my first love.

Christians who have all the time in the world to judge, analyze and criticize others are obviously not running their own race of faith!

God will not lead us into temptation that we don't have the strength to handle; so if we want to move farther, we may need to grow stronger.

Bitterness can prevent the fullness of God's anointing on your life. Don't let people of yesterday rob you of what God's doing today.

God gives us favor, grace and abundance in the areas to which He has called us, so take great care to stay obedient to His leading and calling!

Love can be pretty, pleasant and easy; but it can also be ugly, painful and hard. When we love people in TRUTH, we will experience it all.

I've been working on a "Christmas Communion" printout that goes along with my new book, Our 6 His 7: Transformed by Sabbath Rest! I should have it ready by tomorrow!

I'm done editing and writing for the night! I've accomplished so much today. It feels good to know that I've been a great steward of my time!

Can't help but see all the craziness going on today and quote the famous line from Bill and Ted: "Strange things are afoot at the Circle K."

Based on 1 Corinthians 2.4: My speech and my writing were not with persuasive words of human wisdom, but in demonstration of the Spirit and of power.

My husband is helping me edit my nonfiction novel, Our 6 His 7: Transformed by Sabbath Rest! And he is loving it! YAY!!!

On a serious note: I wore pajamas all day to write. Then I worked out. Now I'm getting back into more pajamas. A writer's life.

I am thankful every day for a life and a chance to make a difference in a world that desperately needs to see the love of Jesus! Mercy! Grace!

The funny thing about being 38 years old is that half the world thinks you're young and the other half thinks you're old.

When we take a stand by faith with our mouths, God watches to see if we make that same stand with our actions. My belief will move my feet!

I don't serve God in my public ministry unless I've served Him in my private ministry: praying, Bible reading, cooking, dishes, laundry...

God is giving me SO MUCH confirmation for the book He has me writing! We are clueless to the rest we have in the finished work of the cross!

I have a birthday announcement to make! I'm almost done writing my 1st nonfiction novel: His 7 Our 6:Transformed by Sabbath Rest.

God is a God of second chances. Not only does He give us the chance to make things right—He gives us the chance to make things awesome!

Super pumped! I wrote 10,555 words in 2 and 1/2 days! Now to write 10,000 more by Friday!

Note to self: There is a BIG difference between "hallow" and "hollow," especially in a spiritual sense.

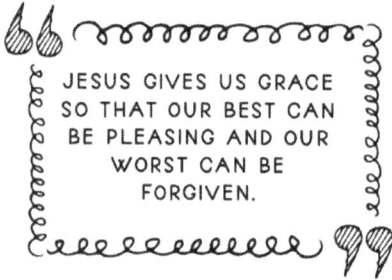

> JESUS GIVES US GRACE SO THAT OUR BEST CAN BE PLEASING AND OUR WORST CAN BE FORGIVEN.

Super tired. My brain hurts from writing all day. But God is good, and He is faithful to supply His words to those willing to seek them!

Having a snack halfway through writing is a must, but finding a tasty, nutritional snack that has very little calories is impossible.

Finally, at the halfway point in my second novel, Bear into Redemption. Chapter 16 was intense and emotional, but I totally loved writing it!

We must think supernaturally: Instead of always responding to our circumstances, we can respond to God, so circumstances will respond to us!

Faith is seen when we take actions according to our belief, not according to the limitations around us. We must walk by faith, not sight.

Struggling is part of our walk of faith, but the fresh perspective gained with every victory makes our struggle well worth the fight!

Fruit not seeded in the spirit cannot transfer into eternity, so we must always ensure that our motives are rooted in obedience to Christ.

Writing may be an isolated calling, but at least I can accomplish the "plans that God has for me" in my pajamas.

God promised me a blessing fulfilled today, and He told me to expect the unexpected. And I can honestly say that I didn't see that coming!

When we are honest about our weaknesses, we can be honest about our strengths. Humility resides in giving both to the Lord.

Don't focus on how you see you; focus on how God sees you!

God will make His promises a stretch for you because He wants you to grow in the process!

Grace is not an excuse to do less for God; it's a reason to do more!

There is nothing more awesome than to be emboldened by God's Spirit to accomplish things in His will that you never thought were possible.

God's grace is not an excuse to live in defeat; it gives us His strength to live in victory. "Your gentleness has made me great" (Psalm 18.35).

My husband barbecued steaks and corn-on-the-cob today, so I could write. He's awesome!

It's amazing what happens when we stay obedient to God's will regardless of the outcome.

Another chapter finished! My second novel, Bear into Redemption, is quickly taking on a life of its own!

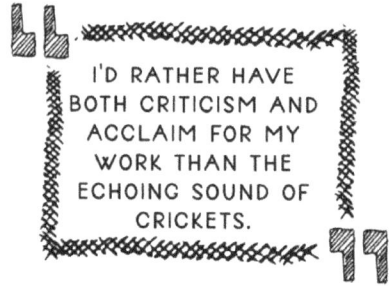

> I'D RATHER HAVE BOTH CRITICISM AND ACCLAIM FOR MY WORK THAN THE ECHOING SOUND OF CRICKETS.

My husband is taking my daughter on a date, so now I get to tackle that difficult scene in my book that I've been fretting about.

It's awesome to be on fire for God, but if we are totally submitted to Him, we will experience an all-consuming fire that never burns out.

A beautiful white egret was relaxing on my fence. I ran to get my camera, but it was gone. It was gorgeous and didn't want to be bothered.

When darkness spreads deeper across this world, Christians will stop picking on each other like little kids and join together like family.

It's not about being strong or good enough to achieve God's promises. It's about relying on His strength and goodness, waiting on His timing!

We are already supernaturally holy because of Jesus and the Cross; the fun begins when we work out that salvation in our flesh (Phil. 2.12).

Our new situations and feelings don't change God's last directive. We respond supernaturally, not circumstantially. Always wait on the Lord!

God gives us signs when our faith is low, but there will come a time when He expects us to believe in His faithfulness alone. Stand firm!

When we lose our hope, it is so easy to drift away from God. Claim God's promises based on His faithfulness alone!

Not giving up sounds easy, but it takes endurance! May God fill you with joy and peace in believing, abounding in His power and hope (Rom. 15.13).

When I stay close to God, I realize that all the pressure I feel is self-inflicted. Jesus carries my burdens, and I can truly rest in Him.

No one is perfect. We ALL need a Savior. The more honest we become about our flaws, the more we'll reach out for the grace and love of Jesus.

When you find complete acceptance in the Father, you will no longer stress about what others believe, think or say about you. Total peace!

Jesus didn't die on the cross so we can DO something epic. He died so we can have a relationship with an EPIC God who moves in EPIC ways!

God can work through our striving, but He can also work through our resting. Learning to abide in Him is the most powerful thing we can do!

Jesus Christ is the ONLY reason that I have access to a holy God. I will never be good enough to enter His throne without the pierced Lamb.

The Holy Spirit is the most influential mentor in my life. He is always willing to teach and guide me in Truth.

People can change their external lives with religion, but a lasting internal change only happens through a daily relationship with Jesus.

Are we willing to sacrifice our peace, so we can hold a grudge? It's not worth our time or energy!

I choose to begin a new journey! My struggling is done. Today, I start walking in God's glory and strength, keeping my eyes on what's ahead!

I can take time to spend with God, so He can supernaturally empower me for my day or I can skip my time with Him and stumble until bedtime.

It is not a coincidence that my two most popular blog posts are about Easter and Christmas. People want to hear about Jesus!

Good news! If you walk this earth, you are a missionary in a foreign land!

I think if we truly believed that we are the righteousness of God through Jesus Christ, our actions would begin to reflect that belief.

Faith is the receiver of grace; unbelief is the rejector.

The best time to seek God is when it's really hard to find the time because that's when we probably need Him the most.

I have faith that God never lets me down even when circumstances do.

I wish Christians would focus on the harvest in front of them and stop bashing the laborers doing most of the work!

Writing for a living can be enjoyable when you have no expectation for profit or gain.

I got another review of Eve of Awakening on Amazon! I really appreciate this line: "The book was fun to read and incredibly imaginative."

We will live an up-and-down Christian life if our faith is based on circumstances and not our faithful God. Stand firm in God's promises!

All three of my kids are in camp this week, so I'm determined to catch up on my writing. Let's see how much I can get done in four hours!

I haven't been able to write on my blog for a week and the world hasn't ended, so I guess I'm okay. Can't wait until my hectic schedule ends!

"Praying for Peace in Israel" has renewed meaning to me now that I've met the people and walked the streets. They desperately need prayer now.

Come to God with your emptiness, and He'll fill it with His best!

Our discernment relies solely on revelation given to us by the Holy Spirit. Our understanding is too tainted to even come close to accurate.

Remember today that Jesus gives life to the dead things in your life and He calls into existence things that don't yet exist! Keep the faith!

Prayed at the Western Wall (Wailing Wall) for Shabbat tonight, thanking Jesus for dying for us and walking with us. Shalom from the Holy Land!

No matter the circumstance, we can ALWAYS proclaim God's promises and His Truth in our lives, maintaining belief in His faithfulness alone!

> WE MUST BE CAREFUL NOT TO RECITE UGLINESS IN OUR HEARTS BECAUSE IT WILL EVENTUALLY FIND ITS WAY OUT.

I want to see life through a spiritual perspective, so I can make choices that influence eternity.

Faith in God's promises when all odds are against you is powerful!

A platform without the Holy Spirit is like land without a spring. If we gain our Promised Land without Living Water, it will become desolate.

Mysterious truth: suffering and glory go hand-in-hand. Suffer in His obedience; share in His glory (Romans 8.17).

Jesus is the antioxidant that terminates all the free radicals (sin) in our lives. Consume more of Jesus and watch your overall health rise!

Our personal lack leads to spiritual abundance. Our natural weakness leads to God's supernatural power!

When we complain about our lot in life, we need to either change our circumstance or our perspective. The Holy Spirit will show us which.

It never fails that when I need a Word from God, the Holy Spirit applies a godly devotional or the Holy Scriptures to my life! Thank You!!!

If you thirst for peace, strength, forgiveness, clarity and love, go to the Lord for He has an abundance of all that is beautiful and good.

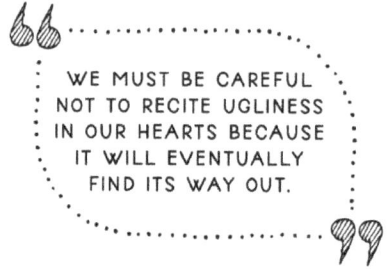

God wants us to trust Him in areas we don't quite understand, so we can learn to walk by faith in confidence, relying always on Him.

Right when I find myself in uncharted faith territory, God provides me with another spiritual mentor.

I will not grow weary! I will not grow faint! I will encourage myself in the LORD! I will scale this mountain and claim the promises of God!

I'm walking in God's faithfulness! I'm claiming His promises! I'm receiving His strength! And I'm embracing His abundance today!

God gives us promises in our greatest areas of lack, so we can build our belief on His faithfulness alone.

I was motivating my son to read more, and I told him reading will set him apart from other kids. He said, "No, God sets me apart." He's right!

God will sometimes allow you to step into an area to which you are not called in order to amplify the area to which you are called.

God has His anointing for your work, and He has His anointing for your rest. Both are beautiful and important realities for a walk of faith.

The Holy Spirit will work on your inward person first, so your outer life is anchored to Christ, but we need to take time to focus within.

Sometimes we fear walking out on faith for God because we think He'll expect more than we can give, but He'll bless a mustard seed of faith!

Continuing our work in an area of lack demonstrates ultimate faith. God will pour out His abundance in our greatest need. So I will believe!

Many of us limit our ability to create something beautiful for the Lord because we are not willing to start in our ignorance with humility.

Sometimes I feel like I can conquer the world; other moments I feel like I can barely make it. So I trust in God's faithfulness alone.

If we are constantly offended, we are definitely not showing love and totally missing the point of grace.

I enjoy editing words of people who have a faith story to tell—it's like dusting off a treasure, glimmering just beneath the surface.

The smile on my face will not leave! I look back to the past month and see that all of my efforts have been for God's glory and His message!

66 RUN FROM GOD, AND HE WILL PURSUE YOU. SUBMIT TO HIM, AND HE WILL MOVE YOU. 99

Very important question! I may ask a couple of times. What is your favorite devotional book and why?

I've been sitting at this computer for six hours. I must get up now!!!

Just talked to a senior in high school who read my book and loved it. She said that I needed to hurry up and write the 2nd one. I agree!

Many times we think we've covered a struggle with prayer, but really the only thing we did was fill it with our nervous energy and worry.

My husband is so sweet! He had to run an errand, and he also came home with a beautiful Easter dress for me that he picked out on his own!

We can love God out of emotion; but when we can love Him out of emotion, knowledge and strength, our faith will thrive through all things.

I want to serve those around me not according to what I think they deserve but according to the highest standard exemplified by Jesus.

The beauty of grace is that God chooses to use imperfect people to demonstrate His perfect glory, love and truth to this world.

God allows our circumstances to change, so we can learn to love Him in all situations. Our love for God is based on an unchanging Jesus.

Our love for the Lord can be the same in the silence and the storm, in the winning and the losing, and in the abundance and the lack.

Via my husband: "All you have to do is keep your eyes on Jesus and you'll walk on things that don't make sense."

God is totaling affirming my efforts! "Never be lazy, but work hard and serve the Lord enthusiastically" (Romans 12.11).

I finished writing another guest post! I love writing for others because it forces me to be extra creative and write about different topics!

It doesn't matter how small the seed; if it is sown in obedience to the Lord, it is better than any prestigious work of human effort.

The people who rolled their eyes at you as you humbled yourself before the Lord will be confronted with their pride when God LIFTS YOU UP!

Just finished writing a devotional, and I already feel encouraged in the Lord! Love God, love writing, love sharing God's Truth!

Making changes in our lives is never easy. If you're not struggling, you're not really changing. Push through until you reach a new normal!

Obeying God's laws doesn't make us holy because we are already holy in Christ. Obeying God's laws reveals our love and unleashes God's best!

Though your position in the hearts of others may change with circumstance, your position in God's heart never changes. You are His beloved!

My wise 9-year-old says his favorite book in the Bible is Revelation because it helps him want to lead people to Christ.

I'm sending my signed book, Eve of Awakening, off to two winners today. I hope they are so blessed by Eve's story!

My husband is taking the kids for ice cream, so I can finish writing a guest post. He's the best husband and dad ever!

> "SOMETIMES WE MUST WASH OUR HANDS OF WHAT COULD HAVE BEEN AND MOVE FORWARD."

My 1st born (9 years old) proclaimed truth tonight! He said, "Mom, when you worship God all you have to do is enjoy Him and love Him." My prophet!

I look at all these beautifully fabulous writers, and I wonder if they write in their sweaty workout clothes like me.

I love it when my characters are emotionally compromised. It makes writing dialogue much more interesting.

I'm implementing a new rule today: I can't work out until I have written on my book. That ought to create writing consistency.

People think I'm insane for claiming eternal life through Christ, but I think it's insane to walk this brief life on this earth and not claim Him.

Believe in yourself when the situation seems bleakest, knowing that Jesus died so you can thrive!

So excited about the book signing for Eve of Awakening tonight. Can't wait to see family, friends and readers at Barnes and Noble.

We have a choice in our time of need: We can respond with grumbling or we can respond with faith. I choose FAITH!

The best use of the Christian imagination is to share the image of our Creator to a world unaware of their deep desire and need for Him.

Doing a bunch of good things in your life does not replace fulfilling that best thing God has for you. Seek God and fulfill your purpose.

We can do things according to our own strength and timetable, but our actions will lack God's absolute peace and abundant power. Abide and rest!

God will rescue, redeem and restore what is completely surrendered to Him. Let go of what little control you have and allow God to reign!

If you are struggling to do God's will, be comforted. God will eventually prevail if you stay in the fight! Take courage and don't give up!

If there were several ways to dwell with a perfect God, Jesus wouldn't have had to leave His glory, entering a dead world to save us.

We can love anyone at a safe distance, but loving people in the thick of their mess takes the supernatural love of Jesus working in us.

Brushing up on my linguistics training for my next book! Really enjoying my reading.

I've been typing all morning, and I just remembered why writing a book is so difficult: It's mentally exhausting and it takes forever!

> **I'D RATHER BE BEAUTIFUL TO THE LORD THAN BEAUTIFUL TO THE WORLD.**

I read over the 1st chapter of my 2nd book, and I think it's awesome! I'm finally getting motivated. Now onto the second chapter!

Every time I try to be righteous by my own actions, God reminds me my righteousness comes from Jesus alone. We are all in need of a Savior.

I love having faith chats with my 9 year old son. His understanding of truth will greatly surpass mine one day, and that makes me so happy.

Don't forget what people intend to use for harm, God can use for His greater good. Let offenses slide today, and watch how God works!

When we remember each day that we are loved and valued, that love and value will influence our response to the people around us.

If we live in our pride towards others, how can we claim that we have humbled ourselves to God? We can't walk in both pride and humility.

Wrote 1000 words tonight and finished the first chapter of my next novel, Bear into Redemption! So excited that Eve of Awakening continues!

I started to get very melancholy, so my husband told me to work out immediately. I feel so much better now! My husband knows me so well.

Your relationship or lack of relationship with God through Jesus Christ continues after your last breath on this earth.

When we start to worry, we're making a choice to step outside the perfect peace of the spirit and walk in the chaotic corruption of the flesh.

Our reaction to correction clearly demonstrates if we are walking in humility or pride. We have just a moment to choose before we react.

Talked to a young man who wants to do something epic with his life. I said small leads to epic, but most people aren't willing to do small.

If God has given you a promise, never let go of it. It's not about your strength, resources, efforts or ability....it's about your WAIT.

Jacob worked 7 years to marry Rachel and the time seemed to him only a few days. When you work for what you love, time means nothing (Gen. 29.20).

When we are real with our own shortcomings and failures, it's easier to overlook the shortcomings and failures of others.

It was awesome to hear my students from 10 years ago tell me, "You always said you wanted to write books and now you are doing it!"

Got to pray with my first reader at my first book signing!

Abiding is staying close to God, trusting Him with all the details of life and believing in His love for us and the strength of His mighty arm.

You must activate your faith in every new storm, remembering that Jesus is in the middle of it and He is mightier than your circumstances!

My internet has been out for a few days, so I can't post any of my work. I'm sure God's telling me to rest from self-effort and wait on Him.

Just finished reading "Humility" by Andrew Murray. It's a small book with big truth. I highly recommend it!

Don't be surprised by the roadblocks along the way. There are always mountains on God's path. That's how we learn to trust His timing and way.

If God is sending you, move in obedience. Your faith even in your lack will create a miracle of God's supply in your life!

When we fill ourselves with God's love and worth every morning, the opinions of others lose their grip over our lives.

Tired this morning because I kept playing scenes of my next book in my mind till late last night. It was like a TV that I couldn't turn off.

God is so good! I have amazing people in my life! And I get to communicate the most awesome message of all—grace and redemption through Jesus!

So I'm supposed to start this whole business of marketing my book. First, release party. Second, book blog tour. I will have details soon!!!

I think waiting is one of the hardest tests of faith, but our patience teaches us how to abide in God.

> FICTION CAN DO MORE THAN ENTERTAIN YOU; IT CAN CHANGE YOU.

Faith begins when we remove every speck of doubt.

Don't be discouraged! God has put you on the earth at this time for a specific reason. Find your purpose in Him and stay strong to His call.

When we think we have "arrived" spiritually, we will cease to grow. I will consider myself the least of these, so I become more like Christ.

I prayed for years that God give me more time to write. He answered my prayer by making me a faster writer. God changed me instead of my circumstance.

When you take control from God, you are an easy target for the enemy. When you give God all control, the enemy must go through Him first.

Feeling anxious about a struggle doesn't help. It only paints a dark cloud over an already difficult situation. Believe this too shall pass.

Righteousness is first an inside job. We believe we are righteous through Christ and the effects of that belief will transform all the rest.

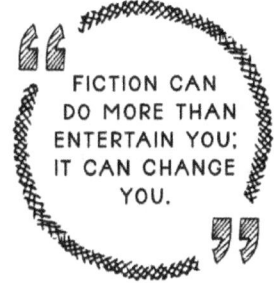

I got to witness to two Jehovah's Witnesses who came to my door! I told them about our righteousness by grace via what Jesus did on the cross.

Belief and love allow us to step past our fear and share Christ with those around us. All we need is more belief and love, and we can win the world.

Super excited! My good friend who read the first (HUGE) draft of my book is now reading the final version. Can't wait to hear her thoughts!

The heart easily commends and condemns itself, depending on our wave like performance. That is why we must base our worth in Jesus alone.

Sometimes God remains silent to see if we'll remain faithful. The stillness exposed our intentions.

I envision and claim God's amazing power and strength in the lives of my children and that image encourages me to always give them my all.

Sent out the last edits on the final draft of my first novel. This book has been 8 years of long and difficult labor. I'm happily exhausted.

Self-denial promotes a safe atmosphere of struggle that forces us to lean into God and grow in His strength.

I'm doing the final read on my book! I'm really excited about how well it looks, and I can't believe this very long process is almost done.

Prayer reaches into the supernatural with seeds of faith that grow into natural occurrences disguised as coincidences, but we know better.

We run our own paths and expect God to bless our struggled efforts, instead of submitting to His path and experiencing His mighty move.

God's love grounds me while His mystery confounds me. He is personal yet all-powerful; in me yet around me; creates me yet dies for me.

Devotionals written by men and women have been a source of spiritual nourishment for some of the most influential people of faith.

God has a perfect plan of peace, but we contribute to the chaos when we walk outside of His will and in our own course of selfishness.

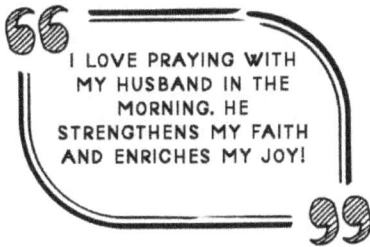

> I LOVE PRAYING WITH MY HUSBAND IN THE MORNING. HE STRENGTHENS MY FAITH AND ENRICHES MY JOY!

I love it when you hear a difficult sermon, but it encourages you instead of convicts you because you have already submitted to its truth.

After our prayer before dinner, my 9 year old added, "And thank You, God, for the imagination You've given us!" He's so much like his mom.

I have a beautiful family to serve, great books to read, a load of discoveries to write about and an amazing God to love. I am blessed!

I desire understanding, but thank God I can have faith! Sometimes life is so messy that I have to trust my way through the rough patches.

Unload the opinions of this world and be filled with God's opinion of you. He loves you enough to be born into a corrupt world to die for you.

I'm learning how to see life in metaphors. Jesus said that He is the vine, door, water and shepherd. What are metaphors that describe you?

I'd rather reach for God through my mistakes than pretend that I have it all together and not reach for Him at all.

When worry, doubt and anger push you, shout, "Be silent, all flesh, before the Lord, for He is aroused from His holy habitation" (Zech. 2.13).

God allows darkness around our circumstances, so we will learn to rely on Him and seek His insight to light our path.

How can we expect our nation to be united when Christians are so divided? Maybe we should share God's love more and our opinions less.

It's interesting to edit your own writing from many years ago. I've changed as a writer, so it feels like I'm reading someone else's work.

I have access to God only through Jesus and His sacrifice. I leave my self-efforts behind because they mean very little in comparison.

"God thunders marvelously with His voice; He does great things which we cannot comprehend" (Elihu in Job 37.5 NKJV). Ask, seek, knock!

Whenever I'm tempted to be discouraged, I remember how much God has blessed me, especially giving me eternal salvation through Jesus Christ.

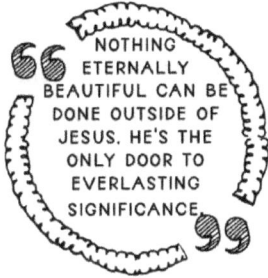

NOTHING ETERNALLY BEAUTIFUL CAN BE DONE OUTSIDE OF JESUS. HE'S THE ONLY DOOR TO EVERLASTING SIGNIFICANCE.

A clearer understanding of God comes with a deeper intimacy with God.

Every day as I care for my children, I remind myself that they are future priests and prophets of the world, and I am honored to serve them.

My 9-year-old son who reads biographies said, "I love reading about great Christians from the past because I know I'll meet them in heaven."

We can learn a lot from Christian leaders, but we shouldn't let go of what God's doing in our lives to copy what God's doing in their lives.

The process is painful, but the result is righteousness.

@Private

What would I be without Christ? I would be what the world desires and praises. Then I would shudder and fade into eternal meaninglessness. I am waiting out of obedience because Jesus is praying on my behalf. I am going through the process of refining.

Sometimes I feel like I will never amount to anything. I feel like my ambitions are too large and my ability too small. Maybe that's why God is having me rely so much on His strength. I'm mediocre at best. I will never write anything worthy of notice. I barely have the time to keep up with my average life. I serve my husband, my kids and keep my house clean and everyone fed. I try to keep up with my blog. When I try to do anything else, I take time from the ones I love. I don't know if I'm going overboard with my serving or not. I have no one to compare my life with.

Father, let us decide together what this life has in store for us. We are in this thing together – Father and daughter, King and servant. Thank You that I have a deep appreciation for my time. Thank You that I am able to be alone with You. Please make me an influence for Your glory. Shine in my life. Everything I have is from You. Bless me ultima. Today is a new day. My struggle is in the past. I walk anew in Your strength and glory.

I realize that sometimes I get into a bitter place. I feel like I've gotten older and have very little to show for it besides my family and walk with You. Help that to be enough for me! Please help me to let go of it all and be content in the Lord. I have no platform. I influence no lives other than my family. I feel like I contribute to absolutely nothing. I'm lost and confused and heartbroken. I'm looking for You in my circumstances. I know You are here, but I feel like You have created a large void in my writing. It's a work offering to the Lord alone. No one responds or shares my writing. I read in Psalms about the wine, oil and bread. I need all of them – revelation, anointing and Jesus. I've fallen into a dark pit. You have urged me to obediently write with no apparent harvest. I seem completely ignored. I need a miracle of God.

———————

I am so sorry for my words before. I was in a bad place. I'm tired of being in that place! I want to be like Enoch – happy in His relationship with God. So happy that God did not allow him to taste death yet. Wouldn't it be so wonderful to die knowing that you are going back to where you belong? I can't wait to be in heaven, but I have a long life of accomplishing God's will. Father, forgive me for basing my joy on the promises of God. I know that they are part of Who You are, but I must learn to have joy in You alone. I don't want my moods to be based on circumstances anymore.

———————

Father, I adore You. You are my heart's desire. I searched for You everywhere, asking everyone where is my Lord. Yet, You have been with me all along. You have been available to me every step of the way.

In Your embrace, I am filled with love, joy, peace and hope. I am waking up early to spend time with you before the day begins.

#YEAR 5

"Look, I have given you authority over all the power of the enemy, and you can walk among snakes and scorpions and crush them. Nothing will injure you" (Luke 10.19 NLT).

The Bible is filled with God's promises to us. The more we read the Bible, the more promises we can claim, and the more power we will have. Jesus says that we have been given authority over the enemy who tries to manifest in our minds, hearts, circumstances and lives. When we confront the evil around us, we must do so with a firm belief that we have the power of God on our side. Since we are found in Christ, we now have the Holy Spirit within us. God's Spirit fears absolutely nothing. In fact, everything trembles before Him. No matter the difficulties facing us, we will overcome and claim the victory with the authority given to us through Jesus Christ.

@Public

We need to love people into God's best, not shame them.

A Christian Leader must be a Christ Follower.

I told my husband what the Holy Spirit taught me today, and he said I water-boarded him with Truth. Ha! Death to self via Living Water.

I would rather expose my soul to the transforming power of the Holy Spirit than live in constant defeat with a battle I will never win.

We are going to make mistakes no matter what, so it's better to be strong in faith despite our mistakes than weak in faith because of them.

I daily encourage my kids to speak blessings and life over each other, not curses and death. Our words are so powerful.

Many times God's word of encouragement to you is also meant for someone else, so make sure to pass it on.

We respect and obey God's Law out of love, not guilt. Our obedience publicly displays our intimacy, not our legalism.

God's grace enables us to live righteously in our imperfect state, but it's not our ticket to live in willful disobedience to His commands.

God has His favor, grace and abundance at the end of your obedience!

Don't try to control the situation. Put it in God's hands and follow the Holy Spirit's leading.

I'm a warrior mom of faith, laying down a covering fire of prayer for my family each morning!

I wrapped both arms around my boy while I prayed for him and felt his heart beating in my hands.

I will focus on God's mercies instead of life's messes.

I enjoy exercising my mind, body and spirit, strengthening the entirety of my existence.

Love leaves little room for putting down others to prove your own point, especially in the Christian leadership.

When we finally let go of our little acts of disobedience to God's will, everything falls in place with ease, power and victory!

We step into God's best with our belief. Our hope reveals it, our faith claims it and Jesus died for it!

Reveal everything to God, and you will find freedom to joyfully and peacefully walk with the Holy Spirit in the righteousness of Christ.

We all make mistakes while doing something great, but God's grace is a glaze that purifies and beautifies everything.

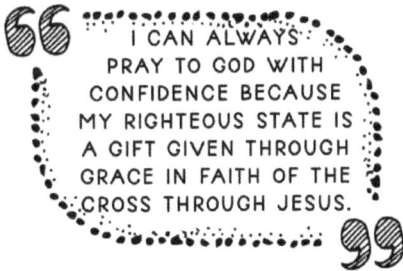

66 I CAN ALWAYS PRAY TO GOD WITH CONFIDENCE BECAUSE MY RIGHTEOUS STATE IS A GIFT GIVEN THROUGH GRACE IN FAITH OF THE CROSS THROUGH JESUS. 99

I find myself lapsing into legalism when I haven't spent enough time with God. I want my life guided by the Holy Spirit, not rules.

The Holy Spirit builds on the smooth ground of humility. That's why God will tear you down in order to build you back up.

When you find yourself questioning who you are and what you're doing, God wants you to cling onto the Truth that you are His and He loves you!

You don't have to justify your actions to anybody. You've already been justified by Jesus' actions on the cross.

Instead of trying to change our circumstances, we can change our perspective of our circumstances!

Instead of enduring spiritual attack, I want to transform the power of that energy into a spiritual breakthrough!

We would save ourselves a lot of worry and heartache if we would simply remember that God wins in the end!

I wonder how I can make today a unique and beautiful experience for my kids before tomorrow begins?

When the little things bother me, I'm not keeping my eyes on higher things. I need to refocus on God, His love and staying humble!

It's funny that every time I meet someone new, I have to warn them that I have an identical twin sister.

I just emailed my endorsements for my debut novel to the publisher! I have been so blessed by five amazing writers and ministry leaders!

Dependency on God is the only way to accomplish the dreams He has placed in you.

If we hate serving in private but love serving in public, our motives may be rooted to self-glory and not love.

The joy people choose to have in this life doesn't mean they have it easy. It simply means they have peace where God has placed them.

Sometimes God leads us into situations that we don't understand because He knows that we'll try to taint His plan with our two cents.

When we submit our lives to the Holy Spirit, we find freedom in being our true selves because God created and knows the real us.

We care more about those things that we greatly invest our lives in. Invest in your relationship with God, and see what happens!

Just finished writing a fiction meditation, and the images created have sapped my energy. I'm poured out but pleased.

Humble me, so I do what is right. Break me, so I cling to You. Expose me, so my motives stay pure.

Align your heart with God's, and your life will automatically be aligned with your purpose.

People submitted to the Holy Spirit will acknowledge, admit and adjust their mistakes. Perfect people don't exist, but the humble do.

> SURRENDER IS THE ONLY PATH TO SUPERNATURAL LIVING.

Draw people by your humility and honor, not by your position and power.

With all the contradictions I find in life and in the world, it is so good to know there is one Solid Truth: God loves us and gives us Jesus!

It has been an EXTREMELY productive day, and I'm still in my PJs!

Remain still and quiet when God allows the enemy to bind your efforts for a time; when you are supernaturally released, shout God's Words of Truth!

When we no longer have our own strength and courage, we can claim the right to God's supernatural power available to us by the cross!

A deeper intimacy with God sharpens our awareness of sin, which causes a stronger need for grace and a free offering of mercy.

If we can wait out the wilderness, God can plant our purpose in the Promised Land.

We take for granted the things that come easily in our lives, but they are no less special than the things that come with great effort.

Seek opportunities to humble yourself because God's glory always follows humility.

Every day is a blank canvas to use our free will to create something beautiful for our Creator.

Sometimes God brings His greatest rains with a storm. Sometimes God brings His greatest blessings with your difficulty.

When you can't muster another prayer for your promises, switch over to praising God for them.

I'm looking for things in my life that I think are insignificant, but I would hesitate to give up if God asked me. I must hold things loosely!

When you are a child, it seems that all you can do is imagine. When you are an adult, it seems that you never find the time to imagine.

When troubles squeeze us, we can either stretch in faith or collapse in fear. Replace worry with prayer and anxiety with God's Word.

It's awesome to worship a Creator who overflows with love, peace, joy and LIFE! Even in the middle of chaos, I claim Heaven until I arrive.

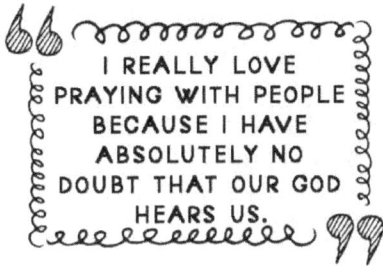

> I REALLY LOVE PRAYING WITH PEOPLE BECAUSE I HAVE ABSOLUTELY NO DOUBT THAT OUR GOD HEARS US.

Sometimes there is nothing else you can do but stare at your dead end and believe in the impossible.

We need to watch the words we say about ourselves to others and watch the words we say about others to ourselves. Words are powerful!

Our limited understanding of God's character will prevent us from recognizing the versatility and creativity of the Holy Spirit's leading.

In a flash this life will be over, and we'll be surrounded by the fruit of our choices. Let's make eternity a major influencer of our lives!

I'm so tired of editing. Why can't a book come out perfectly the first time you write it?

The fact that we get to exist with God in His glory for eternity because of what Jesus did for us is AMAZING! Nothing compares to this Truth!

I pray that my relationship with Jesus would be so intimate that when I write, His life innately bleeds through my pen.

It's better to have no control and be in the center of God's plan for your life than have total control and be completely lost to your destiny.

Children are born with a desire to have meaning. Give them Jesus, and they will have it eternally. Everything else is just a cheap substitute.

There are many ways to know that you are ready for a divinely opened door, but the easiest and best indicator is that you are clinging to God.

You don't need to make sense of all the confusion around you. Simply cling onto God's commands, and they will guide you through the mess.

I don't want God to bless my efforts; I want to wedge myself into the middle of HIS efforts and surround myself by HIS abundant glory!

God, move me, so You can use me today.

My cha tea is hot, and I'm ready to write! I get to explore a unique world of my own creation. Thank You, God, for the imagination!

Never underestimate the power of submission in a person's life. God can do in one second what would take a person a lifetime to do.

We will never be perfect; but if we are honest with our imperfections, God can use them to demonstrate His perfection through us.

We can apply the Bible to our individual lives, and we can apply it to the movement of God's Kingdom on earth. It's a map to all life.

If we are insecure in our faith, our hearts can be hardened to grace because the law has become our security instead of Jesus.

Our intimacy with Christ demonstrates our wisdom, not our choice of words.

God is always pushing me to change and grow. My transformation a year ago is no longer enough for today. I need constant renewal.

The more we pour ourselves out, the more of us the Holy Spirit can fill. Being emptied can be a difficult yet an amazing process!

Many times I wear myself out trying to stay prepared; but if I would rest in God's timing, most things would fall into place on their own.

It is just as important to write a note to a friend as it is to write an article for the public. They both have equal weight and value!

It's hard to let go of our dreams and trust God to make them a reality; but if He establishes them, we know they are part of our destiny.

God came into His Creation, making Himself vulnerable to our disobedience, so He could shine our best and die for the rest.

It's always interesting when I talk to a fellow introvert in social situations. I kind of feeling sorry for us both.

We lose much of our potency for Christ when we find security in people, things, circumstances and anything other than God!

I dislike when people divide action from prayer and vie the two against each other. Last I checked, action is prayer and Jesus did it a lot.

It is easier to hide behind our version of the "law" rather than walk fully in grace, clinging to the movement of the Holy Spirit by faith.

ENCOURAGE YOURSELF IN THE LORD, AND YOUR JOY DOESN'T HAVE TO BE DEPENDENT ON YOUR CIRCUMSTANCES!

We are called to love and serve others. It is the Holy Spirit's job to influence and change them. Our humility allows Him to work through us.

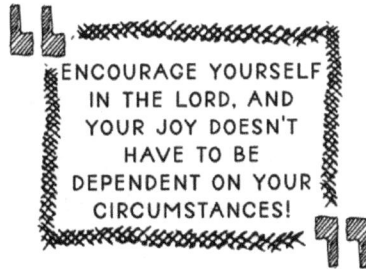

I'm studying the Prophetic Blessing. I want to have confidence praying God's favor, anointing and power over my husband, children and others.

Never make decisions in darkness based on confusion and fear. Always wait on The Lord and seek His comfort, peace, strength and wisdom.

The barista at the drive through seemed confused and asked if I ordered a cappuccino. I told her that I ordered a chai latte. Little did we know that my twin was there!

If we love God more than our purpose, it shouldn't matter what He has called us to be. We would be and do anything for Him!

We will share in the eternal inheritance of every person we serve on this earth for God's kingdom.

We would achieve more for God's Kingdom if we focused on how much we are loved rather than how much we have sinned.

A humble life of service can have a profound effect eternally, and a celebrated life of prestige can have no effect eternally.

When we allow God to do an internal work in us, we will experience the fullness of our eternal destiny.

Solomon began the Temple in the month of flowers (Ziv) and finished in the month of fruit (Bul). You are God's temple, and He is transforming you!

I love my Chronological Study Bible because everything is out of order, yet in order. It feels like I'm seeing an old friend with new eyes!

God is teaching us to be confident in His strength and authority (not our own) because His power is unstoppable and unending.

I don't want to grow spiritually in my own strength. I want to learn to abide in Christ and let Him grow me in His strength!

I must stay yoked to God so my burdens will be light, and I won't burden others with the yokes of the world.

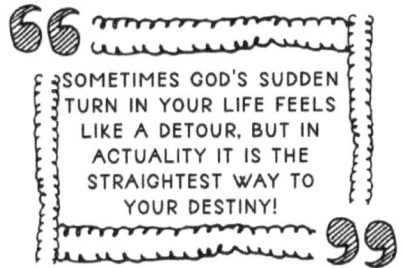

> SOMETIMES GOD'S SUDDEN TURN IN YOUR LIFE FEELS LIKE A DETOUR, BUT IN ACTUALITY IT IS THE STRAIGHTEST WAY TO YOUR DESTINY!

God calls us to leave our comfort zones, walk through uncertainty and claim a new victory.

When I read one book by an author and love it, I quickly read 3 or 4 more of the same author. It's like a perspective download for me.

Trying to teach my oldest son to not only do the right thing, but do it at the right time. Timing is crucial. What a hard lesson to learn!

God must build our anointing strong, so He can lay His glory thick. This takes time, so stay patient in the Lord!

I think I can squeeze in a couple hours of writing while my kids have their "quiet learning time."

Instead of meditating on nothingness, I meditate on a God who is all truth, love, joy, peace and good.

No matter how big or small the decision is, make it a habit to pray and wait on God's approval. You will save yourself A LOT of hassle!

If we can't handle personal spiritual attack, we definitely won't be able to handle the spiritual attack that comes with broader borders.

God wants to fill you with His living water, so He can change you to wine and pour you out to the wedding feast. This takes time. Wait on Him.

Did not want to wake up for my time with God this morning, but Jesus met me at my obedience!!!

Before God will use you to enrich the lives of others in public, you must be excellent at enriching the lives of your family at home.

The Holy Spirit will withhold His conviction when you already know better. We must make our choices according to Truth, not how we feel.

Humility is not down talking yourself. It is embracing your weaknesses while walking confidently in God's strength in your life.

We can build our churches, ministries and lives with great ideas; but without Jesus as a foundation, we are doomed to spin our wheels and fail.

The world says you have to be good enough to get blessings, achieve afterlife, attain value; but Christianity says you just need Jesus.

God can use us to reach a broader audience if we know Him more broadly. Our intimacy with Christ should be deep and our understanding wide.

It is amazing how God can use the non-spiritual aspects of your life (body, mind, personality, money, skills) once they are humbled to Him.

You need to be confident in what God is doing in your life, so you are not swayed by what God is doing in someone else's life.

God reminds me to count the cost before following Him to another level; so when the burden meets up with the blessing, I won't be surprised.

I'm cleaning out and organizing My Documents. Such a pain when you have a bunch of writings all over the place!

When I have my time with God, I always walk away with renewed strength, fresh insight and greater confidence in His promises!

We can fill up on God's Word; so when we speak before people, the Holy Spirit can choose our words from the treasure stored in our hearts.

Everyone is walking in someone else's Promised Land. The key to happiness is learning to be content while in the wilderness.

I love my blog. She eagerly publishes everything I give her. When other publishers won't take the chance, she comes to me with open arms.

My obedience seems to have more effect than my hard work. I think I shall slow down and learn to listen more.

Don't forget to drink from the Living Word! Leave Bibles at home, work, in your purse and use a phone app. So at any free moment, you can take big ole gulp!

Even when you don't understand, stay obedient to the Holy Spirit's leading—trust that your happiness will be found there.

Done writing an article that took me days to complete! Very proud! I've sent it off to the first magazine editor on my list.

I want to be like the woman who gave her last two mites to God. She gave all she had to her Lord: Trust. Obedience. Faith. Love. Selfless.

I love when God has me write when I have no idea what point He wants me to make. He always gives the purpose when I step out in obedience!

I apply Jesus' Words to my family, life and writing. "If anyone desires to be first, he shall be last of all and servant of all" (Mark 9.35).

I get excited about a writing idea, but life intervenes. When I finally sit at my computer to write, I have to somehow rehash my enthusiasm.

> **I LOVE WHEN GOD HUMBLES ME. I PERCEIVE IT, RECEIVE IT, AND ACHIEVE GREATER UNDERSTANDING!**

I may be able to move a rock in my strength, but God can move a mountain in His. I choose to rest in His power, grace and favor!

If we ignore our audience's perspective before we communicate, we will only confuse them. Find a mutual starting point, so your words count.

I don't want to forget my origin: I'm an eternal spirit placed in a body put on this earth for only a short time to fulfill a purpose.

I praise God for not making my path easy. I've had to break, change and grow in order to reach His promises, and I'm better because of it.

I'd rather throw myself fully into God's promises and endure rejection than play it safe and never realize my full potential.

Jesus erases the ugly and sees the beautiful in my life. My mistakes can't stop me from creating good for God because they no longer exist.

> ONLY JESUS CAN SATISFY A HUNGRY SOUL.

As my three-year-old daughter gets on the slide, she looks at her big brother and says, "Wadies first."

We have such a guilt-driven presence in our culture, rather than love-driven. I see it in my own life, but I'm calling it out. No more!

I'm learning to praise in the valley instead of grumble in the wilderness!

Look at your race in life—your triumphs and failures. God only sees the victories, so don't let the mistakes stop you from running full force!

Just wrote this prayer in my Bible based on Luke 7.47: "Humble me double portion, so I may be forgiven much that I might love much."

Most weeks I'm bouncing on clouds of production. This week there is a swamp between every task. But I will press on and finish this week well!

Just deleted 3 paragraphs from my blog post. I had to shorten it up; otherwise, many people wouldn't read it. I must respect people's time!

When we firmly believe we are the righteousness of Christ because of the cross, our lives will begin to reflect our belief!

I learn so much when I write. God takes the words floating in my mind, organizes them, breathes on them and staples them to my heart.

My husband likes to listen to the Bible at night to help him sleep, but I'm an audio learner. While he's sleeping, I'm in rapt attention.

God will bring us to our knees in our own inadequacies, so we may find our strength and footing in Him alone.

We must tie all our emotions, feelings and thoughts to Truth. God is Truth and when we shape our lives to fit Him, we will see His provision.

My son had a dream that he was running fast at the beach with crabs and rattlesnakes under his feet, but none of them hurt him (Luke 10.19).

@Private

I've seen very little evidence of God's blessing on my books. In fact, the journey has been riddled with hard work, dead-ends, denials and a long season of financial lack. But even with all that said, do I still believe the words of He Who is faithful to fulfill what He promised? He promised me many books and people brought closer to Him. He promised me a ministry like a fire hydrant-spread out across the nation dousing out fires and bringing water to the thirsty. God, You are a faithful Father and after years of waiting, I still claim Your words over my life as truth.

I would rather spend time with God than spin my wheels each day trying to have a platform. I will not build a platform. I will not market myself. I will not creatively beg for crowds. I will not waste my time. If God wants me to have a platform, He will give it to me. God can bring crowds and take them away. But I will be content. I will not work in my flesh for influence. If God wants me to have influence, He will give it to me. My load is lifted, my conscience now clean and my path is clear. I will no longer fret or be anxious. I release my intentions to God. I submit to His will. My will is too hard and filled with unmet expectations. God knows my heart. I desire all He wants to give me, but I don't trust my own judgment. I'm done wondering. I am strong, confident and secure in You, but I will no longer move until You give me the word. I must rest in Your power because mine is useless.

I would rather be a servant in peace than fight one more battle for my inheritance on my own. Father, fight for me. I am tired. Release me from the oppression of expectation. I will not speak life or death, but I submit to your authority, strength and strong arm.

Change my desires to aggressively want intimacy with the Lord. I want to see everything through Jesus and the cross. When I feel depression, I must not dig deep into the pit trying to figure everything out. Call out to Jesus to bring you out of the fall.

Lord, I need a deeper relationship with You. I don't want blessings to be the reason why I rejoice over You. Please bring me to Your heart. I want to be filled and surrounded by Your joy, glory, light, love, peace and hope without any strings attached.

———————

The day of crushing. I am alone crying in bed, so I go to my prayer closet, my own Garden of Gethsemane. My help comes from the Lord. I read how God looks everywhere for someone to bring His salvation. But when no one moves, He uses His own mighty arm to get His work done. I have not lifted a finger to move God's promises into my life. I have only labored in obedience by faith. He has asked for others to move, but since they won't, He will move His mighty arm on my behalf. Help the pain in my chest. I feel like I have carried my destiny way passed term, and I need to give birth. I could have aborted it anytime, but I have nurtured and fed God's promises in the spiritual realm and no one sees it. I can't even see it. I only feel the weight of its hope.

#YEAR 4

"Your eye is like a lamp that provides light for your body. When your eye is healthy, your whole body is filled with light" *(Matthew 6.22 NLT).*

The eyes can be used as a metaphor for our perspective. A true, right perspective offers us victorious joy each new day. A faulty, shaded perspective constantly clouds us with oppressive defeat. The only way to wipe the cobwebs from our eyes is to read our Bible, pray and worship. When we read our Bible, our eyes begin to clear up with an eternal viewpoint. When we pray, we cultivate our relationship with the Holy Spirit within us. When we worship, we are empowered with the goodness of God. The presence of God longs to fill us completely. We only need to focus our gaze on Him, allowing God to refresh our minds, hearts and lives.

@Public

God knows I would be a work-horse for Him, so He wisely asks me to wait. I would happily spin my wheels in vain if I didn't learn patience.

I love it when my husband has a word from the Lord for me. He gave me such a powerful verse this morning. I have renewed strength!

Desire the blessing of a godly perspective. When our eyes are filled with light so is our entire life (Matt 6.22), and we see God's goodness.

When our pride usurps truth, we walk on the shifting sands of relativism, an ego driven reality.

Remember God's promises to you no matter your circumstance. He's creating a new solution beyond what you could imagine (Isaiah 43.19).

Innocently pushed print on my book, so I could read it in bed. Didn't fully comprehend the time and ink it would take to print almost 300 pages.

I don't want my legacy to be centered on me and what I'm doing. I want it centered on Jesus and what He's doing.

I'm reading through my manuscript one last time this week before we start submitting it to publishers. Praying for very few edits!

Then Christ will make His home in your hearts as you trust in Him. Your roots will grow down into God's love and keep you strong (Eph. 3:17).

> SOMETIMES THE RAIN COMES ALONGSIDE A STORM. SOMETIMES GOD'S BLESSINGS COME ALONGSIDE A STRUGGLE.

Bilbo Baggins reminds me of Gideon in the Bible. He somehow falls into a grand adventure and he is viewed with more esteem than he feels.

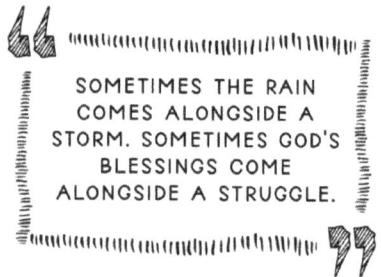

Going to do a little writing, and then I'm off to read The Hobbit in preparation for the movie! Very excited to get a little fiction in.

I will remain content in my temporal circumstance yet stay desperate for God and His will.

The Bible promises a special blessing for those who read Revelation and take its words to heart. I'm feeling mighty blessed (Rev. 1.3).

We can position ourselves to receive God's promises, but it will take a lot of stretching, moving, breaking and changing!

God wants us to find our qualification in Him, so we won't be tempted to feel unqualified and not do the things He has called us to do.

Christianity does more than simply enhance our lives; it changes our lives. Jesus is more than just our Savior; He is also our Lord.

When I force myself to write out of obedience, God always gives me something beautiful to say. He meets me when I'm at the end of myself.

The Gospel is not about being good; it's about finding life through the cross. Sin separates us from God and only Jesus can plug us back in.

I'm trying to get a lot of writing done before my little sis gets here Saturday! I'll have my hands full with entertaining a 12-year-old!

God allowed His perfect design to be corrupted to give us free will and then died for our sins. Free will came at a high price. Use wisely!

I try not to put people on a pedestal of my own expectations. We all need freedom to make mistakes and be ourselves, so we can learn and grow.

I wrote a note in a Bible I read in '08 next to Prov. 13.12 about a promise God gave me in '05. I still believe that promise even in 2012!

So let's not get tired of doing what is good. At just the right time we will reap a harvest of blessing if we don't give up.

I love telling everyone about God's favor, but without obedience to His commands and submission to the Holy Spirit, my words mean nothing.

Writing a proposal for your first novel is difficult because you really have to sell yourself, but I'm believing that God will share my heart!

All of God's fullness dwells in Jesus. If you want it in your life, family and ministry; make Him your main event, not a side note (Col 1.16-19).

Ate an apple this morning and now I'm ready to write! Let's see if writing in the morning is different from writing at night.

Don't waste free will trying to clothe yourself with righteousness. It's given to you through Jesus by faith. Instead use it to grow His Kingdom.

In awe of all this free will God gave me—such a powerful tool that can be used for amazing good. I will not squander or bury it!

You want to speak in tongues? Speak the verses of the Bible out loud. But be prepared to translate because few people understand the Word.

> YOU AREN'T WHAT YOU FEEL. YOU ARE WHAT YOU KNOW. WE ARE THE RIGHTEOUSNESS OF GOD.

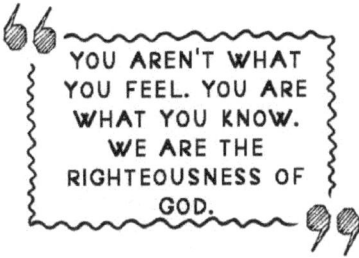

Ever wish a camera could capture how you behave when nobody is watching? Read the Bible. It will reflect the beauty and ugliness of your life.

Authority reveals our root intention: God or self. Self equals pride, which leads to a fall. God equals humility, which leads to honor.

We try to separate God from areas of our lives that we choose not to obey. But God is still there, and His Word still stands.

I'm adding a new scene to the end of my book, and taking out everything that is mediocre. Why aim for a laugh when you can manage a tear!

I won't even mention how long it took me to edit and rewrite two chapters. And I still have four chapters left.

My laptop is not working. Glad I emailed all my draft edits to myself last night. Best way to save work is to put it into the digital abyss.

I'm on Chapter 29. Only seven more chapters to go! My back hurts and my brain is fried, but I will finish these edits!!!

My shoulders and neck are sore from holding my arms up while I type. Who would have thought that editing would be such a hard workout?

People who speak to Jesus directly are confronted with their selfishness. Some choose to love Him from afar, so they don't have to change.

Editing in the women's locker room while the kids do martial arts and gymnastics. I must get done!

When the enemy attacks, you either fall or learn to fight. We need a generation of Christian warriors!

We are all highly favored and blessed, but some of us simply choose to recognize the source of goodness (God) and receive from Him.

If God wanted to give me a comfortable, easy and safe life, He would have just called me straight to heaven.

Any effort we exert to establish ourselves is nothing compared to the powerful force God will unleash to establish us if we defer to Him.

Say, "I'm highly favored, loved and set apart for an incredible purpose by God." Then repeat over and over again until you believe it!

Let Jesus serve and love you today, so you can joyfully serve and love the people He's placed in your life!

My discipline, my efforts and my works all leave me empty. Only Jesus is complete. Only He can fill me.

Thanks to Christ's victory, I don't have to stand in judgment for my sins, so I'm determined to please Him with my love, obedience and faith!

My kids are taking Sabbath nap, so guess who gets to write? ME! Can't wait to dive into God's Word.

You can find God's promises in the words of the Bible, but they're also written across the people, stories and moves of the Holy Spirit.

Jesus took our separation today, so we could be redeemed! If God is calling you to sacrifice, trust that He will bless your obedience!

I squeezed in a couple of hours of writing during kids' Sabbath nap. Now I get to enjoy the rest of my Saturday!

It's easy to be happy for other people's accomplishments and victories when you realize how very blessed you truly are.

I love how God takes something you say, do, write or create and uniquely applies it to another person's life beyond your initial intent.

The more you see God, the more you see your own sin. Since I'm determined to know Him, I need more grace because His light reveals all.

It's easy to sense the negative disposition of others concerning where God is leading you. Don't allow them to distract or stop your vision.

The Bible covers all genres, and the Holy Spirit opens the door to its supernatural and living power. No other book comes close. I'm addicted!

> IT SEEMS THAT GOD LIKES TO BRINGS US FULL CIRCLE, AND THE ONLY THING THAT CHANGES IS US.

Daily brokenness is the only way to live out God's best. Pray for the brokenness of others, but pray for a double portion of your own!

I think only finding excitement in doing things against people's laws and God's laws shows very little imaginations.

I'm meditating, praying and believing on some very detailed and HUGE prayers; and I feel a lot of faith building up!

I love how Job made it a custom to sacrifice for his children. He was extremely rich and powerful, yet he humbly served his family (Job 1.5).

I'm going to take time to be specific with my prayers. It's all done by faith, but I know that my words have power in Christ.

I would rather serve my family than dine with kings. I would rather care for those I love than be spoiled by a world of empty promises.

I find that when I'm a good steward of what God has placed in my life (big and small), I have a sense of purpose and satisfaction.

I love how some of our free will choices may surprise and even amaze God; although, He knew we would make them before time began.

I'd rather be faced with opposition than quietly fade into stagnation.

You want to feel a powerful sense of the Holy Spirit? Spend time with a broken person—grace, peace, joy, love and total submission.

I'm finished writing for the night. I have a powerfully sore throat and a looming achy feeling all over. I hope it's gone in the morning.

I love reading my series of The Preacher's Guide to Homiletic Commentary. There is such rich insight of the people and stories in the Bible.

God carefully arranges circumstances in order for me to make the right choices. Even in my achievements, He has given me grace to win.

God's able to give you the former rain you've missed out on along with the new rain. It's not how you start; it's how you finish!

> WE TRY HARD TO HAVE A MUSTARD SEED OF FAITH IN GOD, BUT HE ALWAYS HAS A WORLD OF FAITH IN US.

I believe God restores the time, recourses and talents we've wasted chasing our own desires if we turn wholeheartedly back to Him (Joel 2.25).

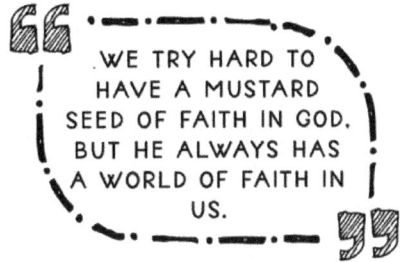

My 7-year-old son just gave me a 5-minute sermon using Proverbs 23.5 on how money sprouts wings and flies away. He's a natural speaker.

I have a vivid imagination; and knowing that God's ways are beyond my imaginings, causes me to pause in amazement (Isaiah 55.8).

When I slow down, I'm better able to embrace all that I've been given.

Your source of struggle will many times become your source of blessings. Wrestle through it and claim your victory!

Calling on the name of the Lord shows relationship, but daily walking with the Lord shows intimacy.

I love cracking open a new Bible! NKJV Chronological Study Bible holds a wealth of treasure for me this new year!

God wants to pour peace into our lives, but sometimes we need to change our perspectives so we are willing to step into His will.

@Private

God is telling me to praise Him even when there are no manifestations of His glory for which to praise Him. I feel God moving me nowhere except to stay firm and unshakeable. I don't know what to pray or I'm scared to pray because I've prayed so long for my book to be published. I wrote it in 2005. It's been seven years. I've lived with a constant need to write this book and publish it, but I'm so tired, so disillusioned. I constantly reclaim my faith and encourage myself in the Lord. But even now I'm wearing and on the verge of tears. Maybe I will wait forever and never understand why. But I trust You, Lord. Help me to linger. Help me to stand firm. If this is a spiritual storm, I will not be moved.

My old computer crashed. Luckily, God told me a week earlier to save my writing and family photos. However, I feel like this is a clean slate for me, like I'm starting on a new level of faith and anointing. I'm humbled and submitted to the authority of God. Before He performs my miracle, I want to be all in and all focused on Him! I want to know the power of God (Matthew 23.29). Jesus' understanding of truth was broad because He loved broadly. He spoke to the multitude, not because of His experience but because of His love (Matthew 23.1).

I believe You, Father. I hold tightly to Your promises. Without seeing my book even considered for publication, I have faith in You and Your Words. Thank You for waking me up early. I want to spend time with You every day. Give me wise discernment. Help me to love others. Help me to serve. You have given me a vision and a people to serve. Please show me Your ways, so I may know You. Please show me Jesus. Help me to wait.

If people are not yoked to God, they may, without realizing it, try to yoke you with the additional weight of their own bondage. Cast off every yoke of the enemy. I am not perfect. I will stumble and fall. Many people won't like or agree with me. I will say stupid things and make stupid decisions. But if I could simply remember to humble myself and give all glory to God, I will be okay. When we don't try to redeem ourselves and fight for ourselves, God will do it – demonstrating His awesome power!

I've been puttering on little faith. I finally realized that I need to dig deeper to spring up more water. I don't know what else to say. I don't know what else to do. How can I pray more earnestly? How can I show You faith? I've waited so long for Your promises—waited and worked in obedience towards the fulfillment of those promises. My dreams are dead. My vision is blurred and the desire in me rages. No answer. No outlet. Only continual consuming desire. Please fulfill Your promises to me. Anoint and redeem me. Shine Your face upon me and grant me Your favor. Pour out Your generosity over me and give me Your peace. Make me Your fire and my writing Your furnace (Isaiah 31.9).

God, I want Your Spirit and my spirit to be one. I want to be totally broken and malleable to You that obedience is easy. I want to hear You clearly without my own influences. I want Your peace and power to resonate in my life and my family's life. I want our wills to be one.

#YEAR 3

"Though a mighty army surrounds me, my heart will not be afraid. Even if I am attacked, I will remain confident" (Psalm 27.3 NLT).

Confidence in God is a choice. When we place our confidence in people and circumstances, our assurance will waiver with the ebb and flow of life. But when we put our confidence in our unshakeable God, we will stand firmly in faith. No matter what the day holds, we can tether ourselves to Jesus, the immovable Cornerstone. In Christ, we are loved and valued. Nothing or no one should sink the joy and peace we have in Jesus. His attentiveness to us is constant. We do not have to be afraid because God is always with us, holding us in His mighty hands. Despite the troubles awaiting us, we can remain confident in the Lord.

@Public

I love getting an answer after wrestling with God! Usually a huge perspective change occurs, but so much clarity is also gained!

Deception helps people live in defeat and ugliness, but the Holy Spirit brings everything to light.

God will break our hearts. When our sinful, selfish hearts collide with His Good and Holy Perfection, they shatter. But it's worth it.

I love celebrating Jesus' birthday. I've captured the heart of Christmas, and His name is Jesus.

When Paul spoke to young believers, his words were plain. When he spoke to mature believers, his words were difficult. Audience is key!

I think when we are experiencing a time of discontentment, we are actually experiencing a deep hunger for Christ.

We can show people a truth, or we can weave it into a story, so they find it for themselves. It's the power of the parable.

May God expose our layers of hidden selfishness, so we experience the righteousness of Job who lost all but wrestled to love God more.

I love that God didn't created the darkness; but since He created the light, the absence of light exists. All good has its absence.

When you outsource one of your responsibilities, don't feel guilty. God will replace it with something much harder.

Base your dreams on God, not circumstance: "Let us hold unswervingly to the hope we profess, for he who promised is faithful" (Hebrews 10.23).

Jesus led the people into remote places in order to do a miracle, and God will lead your leadership into dead-ends in order to do miracles.

When I'm confused by what God is doing, He says that He's working on the "in betweens," like the places in Scripture that are not mentioned.

Don't judge certain freedoms of others because they are probably sacrificing in another area. God convicts us based on our design and purpose.

God has hand-chosen the people in my life, and I want to realize and appreciate their worth and qualities because someone else will!

We need to make sure that our house is in order before we ask God to expand our territory and influence.

I will brush off every feeling of guilt like they were pesky flies and continue to walk in confidence because I have faith in God's grace.

Why settle for Plan B when God has an infinite number of Plan A's?

I am learning to remind myself of God's promises over and over again.

I have a new joy in doing the menial tasks of life because they are easy compared to the difficulties that others are forced to experience!

66 HOOK YOUR AUDIENCE WITH ONE TINY SNAG OF TRUTH, AND THE HOLY SPIRIT CAN UNRAVEL THE REST. 99

Whenever I feel discouraged about where my life is at, I just look at where my life used to be and I become very thankful.

Living by faith looks nothing like the Christian lifestyle I envisioned. Maybe my perspective was rooted in pleasing others, not God.

It is unrealistic to think we can fix a flaw overnight. It is better to find a few crutches that will help us on our path to change.

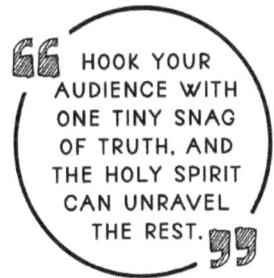

God is faithful, but His ways are mysterious. He knows how to achieve the greatest possible scenario and pack it with drama and suspense!

Worry, insecurity and anxiety are all temptations, and we have no right to indulge them. Find rest in Christ.

See your temptations as opportunities to pursue God. The harder they press, the harder you seek Him.

Faith is like a muscle; it needs to be exercised. Walking in obedience will definitely work that muscle out!

Instead of struggling against a storm, it's better to wait it out. When you are spiritually attacked, be still and know that He is God!

When obedience leads you to a new level of faith that causes fear, you need to dig deeper into your intimacy with God for peace!

Psalm 25 rocks! People are not perfect; but God promises that as long as we keep our eyes on Him, He will protect us from shame.

God commanded the prophets to do some crazy things in order to get a point across, and the religious leaders fussed the most.

I find complete joy, peace and purpose in God, which makes the great sacrifice required to serve Him so easy to do!

I have joy and peace that are not dictated by my circumstances—they are priceless gifts given freely and eternally from God!

I keep preaching some God-inspired goodness to myself. I can't wait till I can share it with a spiritually hungry audience!

When there is no lag time between God's will and our own, obedience vanishes because our hearts and desires are automatically His.

My new writing goal: 24 hours a week for blogs, books and devotionals—all squeezed in during Mother's Day Out, naps and evenings!

The top of a faith-mountain is humbling because you feel God's glory, and you realize that your efforts could never deserve such beauty.

Enjoying a well-deserved vacation with my family in San Antonio! My husband and I are basking in parental bliss!

I want to thank everyone for your support and prayers! God is awesome, and He wants His children to shine!

Our brokenness calls for pain, but the promised joy in our redemption makes the hard times worth it; and we grow stronger with each storm.

There is a time to work hard, sacrifice and push through; but there is also a time to sit back, relax and heal. Now is the time for rest!

There is a peace you gain when you continue in strength but stay surrendered to the amazing will of God.

I made it through another day, and God has been my strength. He is pushing me beyond my capacity, but I find safety in His hands.

I've come to the conclusion that every single life is beautiful, special and extraordinary!

Today will be a day of honor and humility. How interesting that these two qualities go hand in hand.

Joy surrounds the person who follows God's precepts and honors His ways, and shame will not follow the life guided by His Spirit.

There is hope for this underdog because His power is made perfect in my weakness!

I don't understand what God is doing, but I will put all of my faith and trust in Him.

I am activating my faith today, so the promises found in God's Word will be unleashed!

I'm going out on a limb and trusting God in a new way. I firmly believe that His will is better than good....it totally rocks!

I want to please God, and that should change what I think, what I say, how I act and how I live, influencing everything about my life.

As Christians, we should remain confident even when we are attacked because our security is in God and not people (Psalm 27.3).

> REAL FAITH PERSEVERES WHEN NO ONE IS WATCHING AND WHEN EVERYONE IS AGAINST YOUR BELIEFS.

I'm about to spend time with God and His Word! I can't wait to hear what He says. Meditating on Him corrects my perspective with peace.

My life is so full of God's love, goodness and grace. There is nothing more valuable or precious.

The wilderness shapes and strengthens our character, so we handle the burdens that come along with our blessings!

I've been justified, but is my life glorifying? "And having given them right standing, he gave them his glory" (Romans 8.30).

You don't have to fight this battle! God will fight for you and give you His victory (2 Chronicles 20.17).

We are the New Testament priests to the nations, serving the masses with the King's will, glory and love.

Jesus consumed me in His death, spit out my sin and now I stand righteous before a perfect God.

By faith we died in Christ on the cross, so we don't have to struggle with fear, worry or doubt because those things are not eternal.

I want me to be insignificant and my faith to be powerful! May I be lost in a crowd unless Christ shines through me.

God will show Himself very relevant to this world when Christians let go of fear and religious walls but without compromising godliness!

I'm excited to watch God tie all the loose ends together!

I will not start any more books until I finish the ones I'm reading. I just need a week of uninterrupted time. Now where can I get that?

I had a dream that I was a total rock star in heaven. People watched me walk by and whispered about all the cool stuff I did on earth.

I feel God is wanting me to define exactly what I want in this life. I guess He doesn't want me to miss it.

God is complete justice and complete grace. It is difficult for me to comprehend this.

To all the late night writers! Let us hold our chai tea lattes high and begin our imaginings!

I love getting to know my characters first before writing about them.

Being with God has everything to do with our spirits being exposed to His by the breaking of our outer person.

When I keep my eyes on God, I have peace and joy in every circumstance. So simple, yet so easy to forget!

I wish it were easier to pick up the cross instead of the gavel.

I dislike a spirit of judgment hidden under a cloak of concern.

Forty days of writing coming to an end. I added a lot more journal writing into my schedule, which I found to be very fun, messy and real.

God does not give out blessings; He is the blessing. I want to start reaching for Him instead of things.

Jesus is the Life—not works, emotions, intelligence, thoughts or actions—just Jesus. What would happen if Christians grasped that truth?

If God gives a promise, there is no need to keep praying for it to come true. It's better to pray for patience, growth and joy while we wait.

I overcame a very difficult spiritual trial, and all I had to do was BE STILL and know that He is God!

Oh! Happy day! A publisher likes my voice, and the editors think I'm a good fit for their prayer books!

> TRUST GOD'S WORD, NOT YOUR CIRCUMSTANCES. THAT IS HOW FAITH IS BORN.

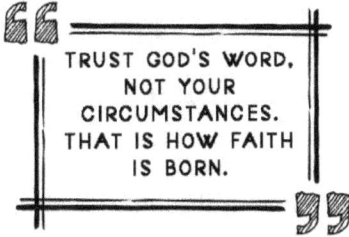

I like using movies to relate spiritual truths. I think they are as relevant as agriculture was in Jesus' time.

You don't have to struggle anymore. You are already crucified in Christ; you simply need to perceive your resurrected self. You are sanctified!

If you don't understand something, wrestle with God until He gives you understanding or peace.

Don't look for verification from others when walking on God's unique path for your life. You will surely be disappointed.

The burden of hope is sometimes heavy, but God's timing is always perfect. Never give up on your dreams!

I got the two most beautiful devotionals in the mail from the publishers that I'm working with!

I LOVE writing prayer devotionals! They are short but powerful insights breathed from the Holy Spirit! Little nuggets of truth!

I finally discovered and wrote down my vision and life purpose! "Communicating the attainable God."

I think insecurity and pride sometimes have the same effect. They both shun people either from self-centeredness or unworthiness.

God makes the fool wise, and I would make foolish decisions without the Holy Spirit's guidance in my life!

If our physical person is under the authority of God's Spirit in us, we can have physical manifestations of Jesus' power in our lives.

Don't pour your best into people who trample over it (Matt 7.6). Simply shake the dust off your feet (Matt 10.14).

When I'm in God's Word every day, He's always faithful to prepare me for what's ahead.

I feel Jeremiah's words: "His word is in my heart like a fire, a fire shut up in my bones. I am weary of holding it in; indeed, I cannot."

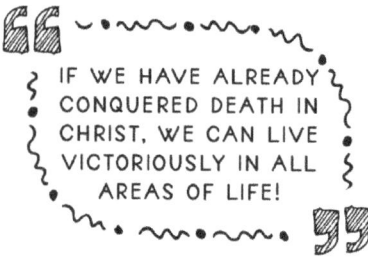

> **IF WE HAVE ALREADY CONQUERED DEATH IN CHRIST, WE CAN LIVE VICTORIOUSLY IN ALL AREAS OF LIFE!**

God matches our heartache with His grace. With all that's going on in the world, I know God's glory will shine!

God loves the process, which is one thing we tend to hate. The process, though, is what changes us, so we should see it as a crazy adventure.

If we avoid actions to harm yet avoid actions to care, we are lukewarm. It's better to be hot for a few, then room temperature for a lot.

I love encouraging people in their dreams. I don't have to run the ball, but I still get to see God's glory from the sidelines.

On my 4th day of writing for 40 days, and I've written a meditation, devotional and three songs. I'm on a roll!

We all have the disease of mortality, but we can stand before God for eternity with the righteousness of Jesus.

Seek God first and see what He takes out of your schedule so you can have more time with Him. You'll be amazed at the peace and balance you will receive.

God burned down David's town just before giving David his kingdom. Sometimes God destroys where you are at, so you can get to where you need to be.

God makes us different, so we can reach the changing world of tomorrow with His love and grace. What is beyond your world of normal?

God made light knowing that darkness (absence of light) would also exist, so He made the moon to shine through the night.

I love that a bunch of little steps of obedience finally equals to something big and wonderful!

We stand perfect before God because of the righteousness of Jesus. And no matter how we fail, we will stand perfect every day until we die.

I like that the Bible talks about another intelligent life form that has been known to communicate with humans. Got to love God's angels!

I'm noticing that there is a fine line between legalism and discipline. I'm praying for more understanding so I don't trap myself.

I want the love of God to power my passion for Christ, so my excitement won't be snuffed or fanned by the changing currents of circumstance.

When God seems untouchable, I imagine a dusty, sandaled foot; and I know that I'm able to touch a holy God through the grace of Jesus.

As the sanctification process deepens in our lives, cling onto grace even tighter. Imperfections become clear, yet we stand perfect before God.

I met a man whose hand was gnarled from throwing curveballs all his life. I was envious that his aged body showed the effects of his passion.

I borrowed some of my husband's faith in me. I love that I can tap into his strength. God knew what He was doing when He designed marriage!

The wrestling is what makes life meaningful. Without free will sin would never have entered the world, but freedom to choose exposes our love.

Who is my God that He would stoop (grace) to know me? That He would agape love me though I will always fall short? I am in awe of His favor!

It seems like every morning my devotional time is EXACTLY what I needed! When you're at the end of yourself, that's when God begins!

Doubt is a temptation to which I will not succumb! It is credited to our righteousness when we believe (Genesis 15.6).

I love watching God show Himself in my husband's life! I get splashed with all the blessings—joy, peace, excitement, love, enthusiasm, awe!

God's love for us is so intense and filled with desire, and He pursues us with passion! We are the center of the most magnificent love story.

Serving, honoring and submitting to others is not a sign of weakness but strength. Jesus had no problem establishing His divine authority.

Christian Bloggers are Internet Anchorites. People come to us seeking a word from God. This is an extreme honor and a weighty responsibility.

> WE NEED TO UNPLUG OURSELVES FROM THE MATRIX OF THIS WORLD AND LIVE VICTORIOUSLY IN THE SYSTEM WE WERE DESIGNED TO OVERCOME.

@Private

I look at other writers and they seem to be so appealing. I look at myself and I wonder, "What do I have to give? What sets me apart? What's my story?" But I'm not special and I have no story, and that is what makes me want to cling onto Jesus even more. In and of myself I have nothing beautiful or important to offer. The only choice I have is to rid myself of me and the world, so I will actually have an impact or else let the burden for more fall from me. The burden wearies me and faith in the unseen is taking its toll. Let me slide into normalcy. I've carried the burden of this book for so long—almost six years. It's hard to always be hopeful and expectant. I've changed and grown so much.

My entire life is different. But nothing about me is attractive, glamorous, confident or unique. I'm so vulnerable to You, God, and my heart aches from years of waiting on Your hand. Am I a fool, Lord? Will you show Yourself powerfully in my life? Will you make a way in the wilderness and a river to flow through the desert land? Help me to humble myself, like a lowly worm even lower than I already am.

———

People see me and the mediocrity. Friends have laughed at me being a writer and speaker. They have never chosen me for leadership positions. The church has looked passed me as if I don't exist. They have placed their thumb of little belief on me. Publishers, editors and agents have ignored and rejected me. I'm afraid to tell them what I see. I am careful not to tell them my vision of God's promises for my life. I'm so tired of being overlooked and patted on the head. God, please break and multiply my efforts.

Please shine Your glory through me, so I can show off my great God. God, give me the words You want me to say and write. Make my spiritual crops manifest in the natural. Redeem all of my faith seeds and pour Your blessings onto my patience. Set me apart and help me to desire only You. Help me not to ingest information and sources that are not of You. Publish my book, so the new chapter of my life can begin. Please, Father, please come through for me by Your grace and mercy, which I do not deserve but will gladly take. Order my life around You and Your purpose for my life. I love You, God. Please fulfill Your promises for me.

Low self-worth and low self-confidence is idolatry because I am worshipping my flaws over God's glory. I will no longer do it. I want to be Your mouthpiece. I want to lead people to You. I want to get my feet dirty for You. God, pour Your glory on me. Shock me with Your amazing blessings.

I'm really praying for peace and contentment. If God's not going to fulfill His promises for me for a while, I want to live without anxiety and longing. I want to enjoy where I'm at and not constantly wonder when God is going to move. I need peace! Help me! I'm tired of chasing a vision so big that it takes forever to ripen. I want Your presence.

#YEAR 2

"This is real love—not that we loved God, but that he loved us and sent his Son as a sacrifice to take away our sins" (1 John 4.10 NLT).

God loves us so much that He sent His Son, Jesus, to die for us, so we could have a relationship with Him. We could never deserve or earn His love. God gives it freely because He is the embodiment of Love. Sometimes, we feel like we have to be good enough to enjoy God's love and goodness towards us, but this is a lie. Once we realize that all of our worth and value comes from Jesus, we will fully embrace God's love despite our flaws, failures and mess-ups. God wants to pour His goodness onto His Children, like any good father would. We are God's Children because of the Finished Work of Jesus on the Cross. Jesus did all the earning and deserving for us. All we must do is learn to freely, joyfully and gratefully receive from Him.

@Public

Life is too short to knowingly make stupid (selfish) decisions. "Teach us to realize the brevity of life, so that we may grow in wisdom."

I love when you wrestle with God, and He finally shows Himself after you humble yourself!

I find it crazy that we can't fit God into our daily lives when He is the One who established our existence and gave us meaning and worth.

Many people in the Bible messed up because they cared too much what others thought about them and this caused them to stop listening and following God.

The world's love is conditional: "If you are good, you will get presents." Jesus' love is unconditional (Romans 5.8).

I don't want to live a life deceived by my own selfishness.

Can we as blessed people walk through a life of abundance and only take what God has for us? What is the Holy Spirit telling you to say no to?

I want to live a transparent life, so I can live the victorious life God created for me before time began!

I love how Jesus laid down His life, but took it up again. Often, God asks us to sacrifice things, so He can hand them back with His authority.

God gave Moses property laws for Israel when they didn't even have land. It takes faith to make plans for a vision that hasn't come true.

I fill my heart with insights from God; so someday when presented in courts, I will not lack for what to say.

What has Holy Spirit made personal in your life today? What has He told you, shown you or revealed in you?

I'm realizing that my marriage is more protected when my husband and I choose to hang out with Christians striving to live by faith in Christ.

Aaron from the Old Testament had the honor to "minister" to God. Indeed, we all have that honor because "minister" means to serve!

I'm realizing that God whispers a vision in our life years before it will actually come to fruition. Goliath was David's whisper.

God calls us to love others with a love we are unable to produce without the Holy Spirit. Left on our own, our love would be self-serving.

"How precious are your thoughts about me, O God. They cannot be numbered" (Psalm 139.17). We should have a good view about ourselves and others!

A RAVENOUS HUNGER FOR GOD WILL SEPARATE YOU FROM THE CROWD.

God showed His glory on the mountain, but His people feared to go. Sometimes the path you fear is the path that will bring you closer to God.

I got to dunk my longtime friend in a horse trough at church in the name of the Father, the Son and the Holy Spirit. It was a blast!

Reading fiction helps me to realize that I have the choice to make my family's story something beautiful, exciting and pleasing to God.

God has us do acts of obedience that are out of the norm; but I realize that's a wonderful way for God to show Himself—out of the norm!!!

The tighter we grip onto God, the further He can take us into our design. We just need to let go of our doubt, worry and fear!

God is the "I Am," and everything else is defined by His existence. We have no identity without Him, and He calls each of us by name.

I prayed today and realized that I'm covered in Jesus' righteousness. I kneeled before a holy God, and I'm sinless and blameless. WOW!!!

Start your day by speaking God's promises. "I'm wonderfully made. I have the power of Jesus in my life. God made me for a special purpose."

We don't have to be perfect, religious or intelligent to receive from God....we just need to be thirsty (Rev. 21.6 NLT).

God's dreams for us are like stair steps: they lead us closer to Him into the image of Jesus.

God's grace pierces the wilderness (Jer. 31.2), and Christians are called to a portion of that wilderness. Take care not to judge a ministry.

I think if Christians understood the fullness of God's love for them, they would be doing the impossible.

You can keep pace behind someone for a while; but when God tells you to pick up the speed, you'd better pass them in the anointing He has called you into.

Sometimes what you're going through will not make sense in the natural, so don't expect people to sympathize or even understand.

Money is used by the world to find peace, joy, love and hope; however, God is a well-spring of those things, and He gives them freely!

God is good, especially when He doesn't do things our way. He is all-knowing, and we struggle with our own limited understanding.

Reading through Chronicles gives me a deeper appreciation for leadership. One king could bring an entire nation to God or away from God.

Genesis starts out with God hovering over Water. Revelation ends with the Bride going to Water. And Jesus calls Himself Water. Thirsty?

I want to love with Agape love (actions), not merely with Phileo love (feelings). Would I be willing to die to myself for the benefit of others?

It's tempting to use our own light (understanding), but God's light is complete. We must let go of our will and follow His leading.

God vindicates us, but we need to pay attention to His redemption plan.

Never let people dress you in their well-meaning, yet limiting opinions. Find your identity in God.

You know when God is about to open the door when all these other "good" opportunities start being handed to you.

Think of what we could accomplish if we took all the energy from our excess and placed it on doing God's will.

Even in the middle of uncertainty, I know God's perfect will always prevails! Now, if I could just make sure that my will is His will.

The Creator says to tell Him your needs and desires. He really hears them and cares about what you need. What an amazing privilege!

Our sacrifice in obedience to God directly relates to His glory and power in our lives.

I'm praying for divine insight for my editing tonight! I'm reworking how my main character meets Christ!

Living a life of transparency forces us to deal with things we'd rather ignore, but there is victory when God has full access to our lives.

Christian leaders are called into dry areas, so Living Water can flow through them, saturating everything with God's presence.

> **WHAT A COMPLETE HONOR THAT GOD WOULD WORK SO DILIGENTLY TO FORM US INTO HIS PERFECT IMAGE!**

The wind can stroke a leaf or bend a tree; and God provides us rest, but He'll also bring us to our breaking point. Both are done with love.

What a complete honor that God would work so diligently to form us into His perfect image!

I pray that God shapes my innate desires to glorify Him.

If our love for others is not filtered through God's righteousness, it can be manipulated and abused.

I'm fueled by faithfulness, finding strength to persevere towards an unseen goal one more day.

Selflessness is when you can give up your desires at any given moment; joy is when you can do it willingly.

I will not claim a spirit of heaviness, worry or confusion. I will keep my eyes focused on Christ and my feet walking in His will!

I stand at His throne, and the world turns around me. I cook, teach, write and clean, but I'm at His feet. Nothing moves me, except my free will.

Lord, help me to work hard within Your will. I don't want to serve spiritually-cloaked idols.

I'm looking forward to writing tonight! God's been knocking on my heart about Ezra vs. Nehemiah!

I can't wait until God lays out my life and shows me all the cool stuff He did behind the scenes. I'm thanking Him by faith!

I'm glad that I'm imperfect; it makes God's grace very visible in my life!

The driving force in all I do is my love for God. It breaks my heart when I don't do His will.

Going to do some editing on a road trip. Here's hoping I don't get motion sickness!

How much writing and editing can be done with a solid week of uninterrupted time? Anyone ever tried it?

I feel like there are three individuals writing my book: The me five years ago, the me now and the Holy Spirit. Now, I call that teamwork!

It is interesting that Esther stayed obedient to her cousin Mordecai even when she became queen of the most powerful kingdom of the time.

> **GOD BREAKS US TO OPEN US, SO WE CAN FINALLY DISCOVER WHO WE TRULY ARE.**

UGH! I just finished writing and editing for four hours and just realized that I wasn't wearing my contacts! No wonder I have a headache!

I got my chai tea latte piping hot, and I'm ready to continue editing my book! It is fun being your own editor five years later.

One conversation can reveal your weaknesses and the other person's weaknesses because each person's strengths expose the soft areas!

It's funny that when you write a book, you want the word count to go up; but when you edit it, you want the word count to go down.

All of God's children are anointed for a purpose. The fear of the Lord should prevent us from judging each other: God's anointed.

I'll eat locusts instead of the world's sweets, Lord. But give me more of Your wild honey, please (Matthew 3.4).

I'm reworking the first several chapters of my novel. Praying for the Holy Spirit's leading on what to cut, keep and change!

God's insights are 3D. Diverse angles make up the fullness of each insight. Different opinions are often facets of a bigger picture.

I'm coming to the conclusion that I'll never figure God out and that my relationship with Him will always keep me alert.

Never work out of guilt. Instead, pick a Fruit of the Spirit (peace, love, faithfulness, etc.) and work out of that.

I find it interesting that Jesus told Peter (a fisherman) to pay their taxes by going fishing. God plants miracles in what we already know.

I love the book of Job. It teaches us that God doesn't want our pretense; He just wants our honesty. I'm pretty sure He can handle it.

The best is always yet to come!

Looking forward to grandparents pouring their energy into my kids. It will be nice to just sit and be still.

My imagination keeps creating illusions that seek to strangle out God's purpose for my life.

What is happening in the physical is merely a manifestation of what is happening in the spiritual, so claim victory in spirit by faith!

Between the place where we receive the promise of God and the Promised Land, there is usually going to be a wilderness which is the opposite of our promises.

We ask God to be bold for us, but instead we need to be bold with God in us!

I'm ready to write! I watered down my chai tea latte, so it would last longer.

> WHEN WE LIMIT OTHERS. WE DISCOUNT GOD'S LOVE. FAVOR AND GRACE.

I prayed over a young woman in the bathroom at Barnes and Noble to be healed of her illness. Let's all be bold tonight!

Jesus is the kingdom of God. Seek Him and all things shall be added!

I want to learn more about Jesus' love for me, so I can be better at sharing His love to others!

God has a particular set of disciplines for the glory He has established for your life.

Holy Spirit's lesson while I was rollerblading: Be careful of the transitions in the road, for they are where you will most likely fall.

There is no fear when you know that you are being obedient to the Holy Spirit—He has already claimed your victory!

@Private

I am absolutely clueless and I'm barely hanging on to God promises. I would have given up years ago if He hadn't planted such a passion in me. I would have gone after easier dreams if He would have let me. I still want to chase an easier path to self-glory, but God has tied me to His will and I cannot get loose.

I am so aware of my lack, of my flaws, of my immaturity that I'm having trouble facing it. I don't even know what I'm doing anymore. I'm so confused. I wrote my book over four years ago. As I read my journals, I realized that at age 14 I felt I was meant to be a writer. At 21 I felt God calling me to be a writer. At 23, God gave me the first-fruit book idea He wanted me to write. I slowly wrote the book in my mind, and the passion to write it burned a hole through my chest.

I prayed that God would take the burden to write a book from me...if it was His will. And it wasn't. I finally finished the book at 29, and I immediately thought that God will fulfill His promise to publish it. Yet, it has been over four years. I've sought publication dozen of times, but I was rejected each time. God has pretty much told me to sit on it wait.

Wait. Wait. Wait.

I thought I was waiting to become good enough, but I realize that I will never be good enough, strong enough or ready enough. So why am I waiting if I need grace anyways? I think God wants me to be happy. The hardest thing that I'm learning to do is be content and happy in a constant state of anticipation. It is so hard, and I don't want to anticipate another day.

I prayed last night for God to stop the waiting. Either way— published or not — I don't care. Just stop the waiting. I can't do it anymore. I feel like I've obediently walked into a brick wall and I'm waiting for God to move it. But He hasn't. I think if I pray the right way or do the right things, He will move it. He doesn't.

———————

I waited today for God to do a miracle, but it hasn't happened. I won't be surprised if it doesn't. Actually, I'm pretty sure it won't. That is how disenfranchised I am about this whole situation. I'm done pretending to be happy and strong and prepared.

I am happy as a mom. I am happy as a wife. I am happy as a Christian. I'm miserable and confused as a writer. I'm done writing. I'm not one of those writers who writes for personal benefit. I would just keep a journal if that were true. I write for an audience; otherwise, what is the point?

I wrote nonchalant for God for three years on a blog no one read. It wasn't until people started reading that I put more effort into it. I write for an audience, to make a difference, to communicate a truth.

I've been following God's voice down a path of confusion, and I don't think I can make it out. Sometimes I want to fold up my computer screen, say goodbye to writing and live my life without waiting on God to fulfill His promises. What if I'm a fool? I could be a fool on much easier terms.

I'm disillusioned and exhausted, and I can't take another step of blind faith. God do You hear me? I'm not pretending to be strong anymore. I will boast in my weaknesses so Your power can rest on me. I am incapable of doing what You ask. Please, Father, make the waiting stop. I'm good either way. Don't publish my book. Don't let me be a writer. I will continue to be the best mom and wife – just pay up or bail out. I cling tightly to You, Father, but that's all I can do. I can no longer trudge forward. I am done.

I prayed for trust today – trust based on no proof. I want to believe God loves me with a love that transcends my current understanding. I want to trust and have confidence in the promises He has given me without verification. I love Him so much, and I want Him to know that I will walk empty handed through the fire for Him. I will jump off a cliff if He tells me to because I know that He will catch my fall or allow me to heal from my injuries. I will trust God with the pains I occur in this life.

God leads me into battles knowing I will get hurt, but He allows me to heal and become stronger. God, I will not doubt you anymore. I leap blindly for You. The Bible is filled to overflowing with Your promises to me, and I take You at Your Word. You will bless me more than I can possibly fathom, and You will shoot Your glory through me so I can experience heaven on earth.

Heaven is all around me. I feel the angels crying out Your glory. I want to take part of the grand symphony in Your honor. Let it be a credit to my faith that I sing along with a heavenly concert that I cannot see nor hear, but I know the music is all around me. Your glory can't help but soak up praise, and I want to be a part of that joy and majesty. I want to experience thick happiness of heaven here on this corrupted world.

Let me be a willing player in the beauty of this life that You have created throughout time. Let me feel the significance of my role in Your creation without proof or understanding. Please plant inside of me a trust and faith that can only come from You. Pour out Your favor on me. Give me the trust that Jesus had when He willingly went to the cross though He didn't want to. I trust that You have a future and a hope for me, and that You want to prosper and bless me.

Keep me broken and malleable. Humble me and teach me. I want to gain wisdom and a healthy fear of Your greatness. I happily give up my desires because I want what You desire for me more. Show Yourself to me. I walk by faith and I trust Your hand, but I desire to see You move mightily in my life.

———————

I realized that the reason I am consumed by negative feelings is because I'm not abiding in God enough. When the negative feelings come on strong, I need to abide more. I discovered that I wasn't accepting God's love, and that is where this 1 John 4.10 verse comes in. My love for God is nothing in comparison with His love for me.

All these years I've been freely accepting God's correction and admonishing. I change what He tells me to change and I continuously humble myself to His hand. However, I have not been accepting His love. He had to give me a verse of encouragement twice before I would fully accept His love for me.

Finally, today I just abided in Him and let Him fill me with His love. I didn't think about all the mistakes I had made, all of my failures, all of the things I needed to change, what I needed to do to become stronger for Him. I just let Him love me as a daughter – not for who I am, but for who He is. His love transcends all human understanding, and I think I'm only scraping the surface.

#YEAR 1

"Go and celebrate with a feast of rich foods and sweet drinks, and share gifts of food with people who have nothing prepared. This is a sacred day before our Lord. Don't be dejected and sad, for the joy of the LORD is your strength!" (Nehemiah 8.10 NLT).

God loves celebration! We have so much to be thankful for, but sometimes we forget about the abundance of blessings God gives us each day because we focus so much on what we don't have. But truly if we have accepted Jesus Christ as our Lord and Savior, we know that we will live for eternity with God in heaven. This is the ultimate reason to celebrate! Knowing that the Lord is with us each day—in the good times and bad—gives us supernatural strength. We are not walking this life alone. We have a Helper—the Holy Spirit—within us. We have a Savior praying for us. And we have a God Who is rooting for us.

@Public

God is my rock, and I am His living stone. I don't want to do anything in vain. Guide my steps, so I can live pleasing to You.

I've been eating a lot of humble pie with my pumpkin pie. Hopefully, I will digest everything the Holy Spirit is teaching me.

Wondering how many Christians are truly yoked to Jesus and not the enemy. Wouldn't we exhibit the power of the resurrection more?

What do the most influential Christian women and men have in common? Heaven eyes—a good understanding of the other realm!

I don't understand people who say that they are open to all beliefs, but then they go and pick on Christians. Why are we the exception?

Whenever I watch a movie, I know God can do better in my life. He gives His kingdom to those who love Him.

> IF WE LIVE TRANSPARENT LIVES, THEN THE MOST BEAUTIFUL AND AMAZING THING IN ALL OF EXISTENCE WOULD BE MORE EASILY SEEN.

There seems to be an outbreak of humility around me, and I love it! God is about to move mightily!!!

I like the image of tearing one's clothes found in the Bible. It is such a beautiful symbol of brokenness before God.

I asked my friend if she accepted Jesus in her heart, and she said yes. That's a load off!!!

Just finished teaching One on One with God. I pray that God brings to life a seed that was planted.

Saw a man with a tattooed sleeve lifting his arm up to God in worship at church. He reminded me of King David. What a beautiful sight!

Start digging ditches in the valley or making jars; so when God pours down His blessings, you'll be able to hold all of it (2 Kings 3 and 4).

Praying for and expecting a confirmation. I can't wait to see God do His thing!

I'm trying to find appropriate, God-centered balance while multi-tasking. Busyness has to be effecting my hearing the Holy Spirit.

Feel like God has opened my eyes to the beauty all around me. Hubby would sacrifice everything for me and my boys are unfolding books.

With regard to my New Year's resolution, I'm going to study scripture that gives promises of joy. I want to understand God's joy (Neh. 8.10).

How do you talk about your intimate relationship with God in a way that's palatable to others?

My kids remind me of why God created us: they bring joy and pain, but the beauty of their lives is so worth it all.

I think pride does more destruction in insecure people because it hides and is harder to detect. I hate pride because it has so many faces.

Two questions: How do you live victoriously while continually being humbled? How do you live like a child, while covered with responsibility?

WE CAN REST IN GOD AND GIVE HIM ROOM TO WORK!

Being a fulltime mom is physically and emotionally draining and spiritually isolating. No wonder I love my time with God.

I will be finished reading the Bible tonight! I started less than a year ago. It feels good, and I've learned so much. I can't wait to read it again!

@Private

I'm putting my writing on my blog, and I'm feeling vulnerable, nervous and scared. What if I'm doing the wrong thing? Who and what gives me the right to discuss spiritual themes? Should I feel happy that God has promised me publication and rely on His promise or should I be discouraged that my platform is completely void? I need to put my trust in God and not my circumstances. God has been teaching me to praise Him for His promises before they come to pass. So I will do that! I will praise Him and try not to be insecure and embarrassed that all odds are against me to publish. It will clearly be a God-given miracle. Help me to praise You, Father. Please show me what You want me to write next.

To perceive, recognize and understand the wonders of His Person – I want that. I want to be able to take in all Your wonders, so I may fully understand how blessed and lucky I am to be a Christian. I think that the disciples saw and experienced Jesus every day, and they may have taken Him for granted. That is exactly where I am at right now. I've taken the beauty and majesty of Christ for granted. Instead of saying, "I want you to love me the best. I want to be your favorite," I should realize the humbling truth that it is only because of Jesus that I get to even call myself known by Christ. Thank You, Jesus, for redeeming me!

I wish I had more time. Someday I'll have no little souls needing me, and I'll have all the time in the world. I'll be old and wonderfully weighed down with a life full of memories. I will wish I could hold my babies to my heart once more and with my lips give them continuous kisses on their cheeks. They are grasping onto me with little hands, engulfing themselves in the feeling of me. They don't understand how complex and fragile the relationships of this world are. They only comprehend the love they feel now...the love of a mother. And I want to give them an abundance of that love before my time as their first true love is up. I don't want to write, edit, serve in ministry, workout or enjoy entertainment if it takes all my time, uses all my energy and leaves no room for my family and my God! Take it away! Take the passion, giftings and abilities away if I have nothing left!

I feel like God wants me to write Bible principles in a way that will help our current culture to understand them. I'm very imaginative and my mind is constantly creating stories of spiritual grandeur. I believe He wants me to write principles from Bible stories and reveal God's glory through my storytelling. I'm very excited about it. It seems so fun to me—almost like entertainment with a dash of hope. Can't wait!

I'm really hard on myself, and that pressure presses on my children. I think there is nothing wrong with having high expectations, but I need to add just as much joy to it or what is this life for? God wants us to work hard, but He wants us to enjoy ourselves. I find it difficult to enjoy myself. I'm blessed beyond belief and I love my life as a wife and mom, but I can't be so disciplined and melancholy all the time.

I'm begging God to teach me to praise His goodness in front of my children, to show them the joy that He gives me. I'm worried that publishing a book will make me even more disciplined, and, honestly, I've disciplined my life enough. There's nothing wrong with lots of discipline, but nobody wants to read (or live) a story about a woman who has disciplined the joy out of her family's life.

I'm praying God teaches me. How can I continuously renew my mind and allow Him to transform me without feeling the weight of change? How can I be the writer and woman of God that I'm called to, but still be a fun-loving, free-spirited wife and mother I'm called to be?

I feel like I need to let go of worry and anxiety that I've been holding onto. How can I be childlike, yet live with the burden of a high calling? God has to give me grace. I have children, and I want to ensure that they like being around me. I want them to want my companionship when they get older. I want them to like me as a person. I want them to love being with me.

Lord, I want to not only love my kids – I want to make life wonderful for them. I want to show them how to be disciplined, yet carefree. Lord, help me to cast all my cares on You, so my children don't feel their burden. Show me how to love each one of them how they each need to be loved. My time with them is so limited. I feel it slipping away, but they are still so young. Why does life go by so fast? Why is life so fragile? Teach me to number my days. I know You have great plans for me, but I want to enjoy my family along the way.

Help me to praise You more in front of my children. Let them hear Your praises; so when they find themselves in darkness, they know how to claim Your light!

#EPILOGUE

When I read through the public and private words of my faith, I definitely feel the struggle between doubt and belief. It is a hard thing to obediently wait in the caves of your dreams and trust God will make a way when there is no way. However, I get a sense that as the years go by, faith finally begins to take root in my heart and soul, overshadowing disbelief. This faith took a very long time to produce, which is maybe why Jesus said that we only need a mustard seed of it.

The other thing I notice when reading over these last ten years is that as a mother, God led me slowly when my kids were young (Isaiah 40.11). I remember wanting to do so much for God, but He always held me back. Now I see why. The time I had with my family when my kids were young was so precious and fleeting. I am glad I trusted God and kept my role as mother a priority. I wouldn't exchange the years I spent in the thick of motherhood for all the books in the world.

Finally, I see that I shielded a lot of my struggle from my public faith, which I think was healthy for the most part. Like a mother, when I went before the public eyes, I wanted to ensure that I was focusing on encouraging them (and in return myself), not spilling out my own woes. People are weighed down by their struggles already, and they don't need me adding to their burden. When I did wrestle with my faith, I did it in private before God. My husband felt my struggle, as well, and he would endeavor to encourage me and pour belief into me.

Now, I hope to inspire others who are walking through the wilderness of their promises. Yes, the journey is long, but God is producing faith in us. Will we believe in His Word or our circumstances? Will we choose to live by faith or sight? Jesus wondered if anyone on earth would have faith when He came back (Luke 18.8). I hope that He will. I know He will find faith in me, and I pray that after reading this book, He will find it in you.

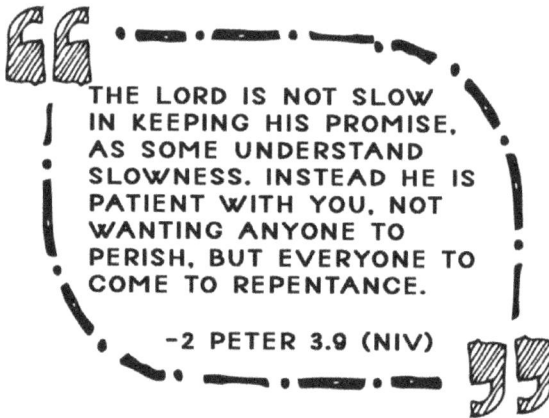

> **THE LORD IS NOT SLOW IN KEEPING HIS PROMISE, AS SOME UNDERSTAND SLOWNESS. INSTEAD HE IS PATIENT WITH YOU, NOT WANTING ANYONE TO PERISH, BUT EVERYONE TO COME TO REPENTANCE.**
>
> **-2 PETER 3.9 (NIV)**

If your faith has been encouraged, please leave a review on Amazon for others to read. You can find my other fiction and nonfiction books at Amazon or my blog, www.alisahopewagner.com. I pray that you continue to live a life of faith, especially when it doesn't make sense.

- alisa

www.ingramcontent.com/pod-product-compliance
Lightning Source LLC
LaVergne TN
LVHW011329080426
835513LV00006B/257